mate Sauce & Dressing Cookbook

Dishes, Volume 2

Olivia Bennett

Published by B&H Publishing Group, 2025.

While every precaution has been taken in the preparation of this book, the publisher assumes no responsibility for errors or omissions, or for damages resulting from the use of the information contained herein.

THE ULTIMATE SAUCE & DRESSING COOKBOOK

First edition. February 19, 2025.

Copyright © 2025 Olivia Bennett.

ISBN: 979-8230212898

Written by Olivia Bennett.

Table of Contents

To all the home cooks, food lovers, and kitchen experimenters who believe that the right sauce can turn a simple meal into something extraordinary.

To my family and friends, whose love and shared meals have inspired my passion for flavor.

And to the chefs, past and present, who have taught us that cooking is not just a skill but an art.

May your tables always be filled with good food, great company, and the perfect sauce.

Introduction: Unlocking the Magic of Sauces and Dressings

Sauces and dressings are the unsung heroes of the culinary world. They are the bridge between a good dish and a truly great one, capable of transforming simple ingredients into complex, flavorful creations. Whether it's the velvety richness of a hollandaise sauce, the bright tang of a vinaigrette, or the bold spice of a barbecue glaze, sauces and dressings bring harmony, depth, and excitement to the table.

In this chapter, we'll explore why sauces and dressings are indispensable to cooking, the science behind balancing flavors, and the essential tools and ingredients needed to master the art of sauce-making. By the end, you'll have a foundational understanding of how to unlock the magic of sauces and dressings, setting the stage for culinary creativity.

Why Sauces and Dressings Are the Heart of Every Great Dish

1. Enhancing Flavor and Texture

A perfectly made sauce or dressing can enhance a dish by adding complementary flavors, contrasting textures, and visual appeal. They bring balance to every bite, ensuring that no element feels flat or overwhelming.

Key Roles of Sauces and Dressings:

- Adding Moisture: Creamy or brothy sauces keep dishes moist, especially proteins like chicken or fish.

- Enhancing Flavor: A tangy vinaigrette can brighten a salad, while a rich gravy can amplify the savoriness of a roast.

- Creating Contrast: Sweet sauces balance spicy dishes, and acidic dressings cut through rich, fatty foods.

- Binding Ingredients: Dressings coat salads evenly, while sauces hold pasta and grains together.

Example: Imagine grilled chicken breast—by itself, it's flavorful but plain. Add a lemon butter sauce, and the dish becomes vibrant and luxurious.

2. The Transformative Power of Sauces and Dressings

Sauces and dressings elevate even the simplest meals:

- Pasta: A basic bowl of spaghetti transforms with a rich marinara or creamy Alfredo sauce.

- Salads: A handful of greens become a gourmet dish with the right dressing.

- Meats: A perfectly grilled steak reaches new heights with a peppercorn sauce or red wine reduction.

Pro Tip: A well-made sauce can act as a safety net, salvaging overcooked proteins or under-seasoned vegetables by adding moisture and flavor.

3. Cultural Significance

Around the world, sauces and dressings are integral to cultural cuisines:

- France: Known for the five mother sauces, which form the basis of classic French cooking.

- Italy: Pasta sauces like marinara, pesto, and carbonara are culinary staples.

- Asia: Soy sauce, miso, and fish sauce are foundational in creating bold, umami-packed dishes.

- Mexico: Salsas and mole sauces add depth and spice to dishes.

Example: A French béchamel and an Italian Alfredo sauce share common elements but reflect different culinary traditions.

The Balance of Flavors: Sweet, Salty, Sour, Bitter, and Umami

1. Understanding the Five Basic Tastes

Balancing flavors is at the heart of crafting sauces and dressings. By understanding how each taste interacts, you can create complex and harmonious flavors.

The Five Tastes:

1. Sweet: Adds softness and rounds out acidic or bitter elements.
- Examples: Honey in vinaigrettes, sugar in tomato sauce.
2. Salty: Enhances other flavors and provides balance.
- Examples: Soy sauce, anchovies, or a pinch of kosher salt.
3. Sour: Cuts through richness and adds brightness.
- Examples: Lemon juice, vinegar, or tamarind.
4. Bitter: Offers depth and complexity, balancing sweetness.
- Examples: Mustard, dark chocolate, or coffee.
5. Umami: Provides savoriness and a sense of fullness.
- Examples: Parmesan cheese, miso, or Worcestershire sauce.

2. How to Balance Flavors in Sauces and Dressings

Achieving balance requires understanding how tastes complement or contrast each other:

- Sweet and Salty: Balances richness; think honey mustard dressing.
- Sour and Sweet: Creates contrast; imagine sweet and sour sauce.
- Bitter and Umami: Adds depth; consider dark soy sauce paired with garlic.

Pro Tip: Always taste as you go, adjusting with small amounts of ingredients to achieve harmony.

3. Using Aromatics and Spices

While the five tastes form the foundation, aromatics and spices bring character to sauces and dressings:

- Aromatics: Onions, garlic, shallots, and herbs like thyme and rosemary.
- Spices: Cumin, paprika, turmeric, and chili powder add warmth and complexity.
- Acids: Vinegars (balsamic, red wine, apple cider) and citrus juices are indispensable for balancing richness.

Example: A simple tomato sauce becomes extraordinary with garlic, basil, and a pinch of red pepper flakes.

Tools, Techniques, and Pantry Essentials for Making Perfect Sauces and Dressings

1. Essential Tools

Having the right tools makes sauce and dressing preparation efficient and enjoyable.

Must-Have Tools:

- Whisk: For emulsifying vinaigrettes and creating smooth sauces.

- Blender or Food Processor: Perfect for pureeing pestos, salsas, and creamy dressings.

- Saucepan: A heavy-bottomed pan ensures even heat distribution for roux-based or reduction sauces.

- Strainer or Fine Mesh Sieve: Removes solids for velvety-smooth sauces.

- Immersion Blender: Ideal for pureeing directly in pots or bowls.

- Measuring Spoons and Cups: Precision is key for balancing flavors.

Pro Tip: A silicone spatula is excellent for scraping every bit of sauce from a pan or bowl.

2. Pantry Essentials

Stocking your pantry with versatile ingredients ensures you're always ready to whip up a delicious sauce or dressing.

Basic Ingredients for Sauces and Dressings:

- Oils: Olive oil, neutral oils (canola, grapeseed), and sesame oil.

- Vinegars: White wine, red wine, balsamic, rice, and apple cider vinegar.

- Dairy: Butter, cream, and cheese (Parmesan, blue cheese).

- Aromatics: Garlic, onions, shallots.

- Spices: Salt, pepper, chili flakes, cumin, and paprika.

- Sweeteners: Honey, maple syrup, sugar.

- Thickeners: Flour, cornstarch, egg yolks.

Specialty Ingredients:

- Asian Pantry Staples: Soy sauce, miso, hoisin, fish sauce, and mirin.

- Mediterranean Staples: Capers, olives, anchovies.

- Umami Boosters: Tomato paste, Worcestershire sauce, nutritional yeast.

Pro Tip: Keep fresh herbs like parsley, cilantro, and basil on hand to brighten and garnish dishes.

3. Techniques for Perfect Sauces and Dressings

1. Whisking Emulsions:

- Gradually add oil to vinegar or citrus juice while whisking to create a stable vinaigrette.

2. Reducing Liquids:

- Simmer sauces to concentrate flavors and thicken naturally.

3. Thickening with Roux:

- Cook equal parts butter and flour, then whisk in liquid (milk, stock) for a creamy base.

4. Tempering Eggs:

- Gradually add hot liquid to beaten eggs to prevent curdling in custard-based sauces.

5. Blending:

- Use a blender for silky textures in pestos, nut-based dressings, and pureed sauces.

Pro Tip: Practice patience—perfecting textures and balances often takes time and adjustments.

Closing Thoughts

Mastering sauces and dressings is a journey that begins with understanding their transformative power, balancing flavors, and using the right tools and ingredients. This foundational knowledge will empower you to create dishes that delight the senses and showcase your culinary creativity. As you move through the chapters of this book, you'll discover the endless possibilities sauces and dressings offer, from simple vinaigrettes to complex reductions. Let's unlock the magic together and take your cooking to new heights!

Chapter 1: Classic Mother Sauces

The world of sauces owes much of its richness and versatility to the foundation laid by the five French mother sauces: béchamel, velouté, espagnole, hollandaise, and tomato sauce. These sauces, codified by French chef Auguste Escoffier in the early 20th century, form the basis for countless culinary creations across cuisines. By mastering these sauces, you gain a toolkit to craft a vast array of dishes, from comforting casseroles to sophisticated entrées.

In this chapter, we'll dive into the history and importance of these sauces, provide step-by-step instructions to make each one, and explore modern variations and their uses in contemporary cooking.

The Significance of the Mother Sauces

1. Why Are They Called "Mother Sauces"?

The term "mother sauces" refers to their foundational role in cuisine. Each sauce serves as a "parent" to a family of derivative sauces, which are created by adding additional ingredients or modifying the base sauce.

Key Features of Mother Sauces:

- Versatility: They are the starting point for countless other sauces.

- Simplicity: Made with a few basic ingredients, they demonstrate the elegance of French cooking.

- Adaptability: These sauces can be modified to suit different cuisines and dishes.

2. The Legacy of Escoffier

Auguste Escoffier, often called the "father of modern French cuisine," formalized the concept of mother sauces in his book *Le Guide Culinaire*. These sauces streamlined and organized the approach to sauce-making, allowing chefs to create complex flavors efficiently.

The Five Mother Sauces

1. Béchamel: The Creamy Classic

Béchamel, also known as white sauce, is a simple yet luxurious sauce made from milk, butter, and flour. It is often used as a base for creamy dishes and baked gratins.

Ingredients:

- 2 tablespoons butter

- 2 tablespoons all-purpose flour

- 2 cups milk

- Salt, white pepper, and a pinch of nutmeg

Instructions:

1. Make a Roux: Melt butter in a saucepan over medium heat. Add flour and whisk continuously for 2-3 minutes until the mixture is smooth and pale.

2. Add Milk Gradually: Slowly pour in the milk, whisking constantly to prevent lumps.

3. Simmer and Season: Bring to a gentle simmer, stirring often, until the sauce thickens (5-7 minutes). Season with salt, white pepper, and nutmeg.

Derivative Sauces:

- Mornay Sauce: Add grated cheese (e.g., Gruyère or Parmesan) for a cheesy variation.

- Cream Sauce: Enrich with cream for an ultra-luxurious texture.

Uses in Modern Cooking:

- Lasagna, macaroni and cheese, croque monsieur, and vegetable gratins.

2. Velouté: Silky and Subtle

Velouté is a light and delicate sauce made from a roux and white stock (chicken, veal, or fish). Its name comes from the French word for "velvety."

Ingredients:

- 2 tablespoons butter

- 2 tablespoons flour

- 2 cups white stock (chicken, veal, or fish)

- Salt and white pepper

Instructions:

1. Make a Roux: Melt butter in a saucepan and whisk in flour, cooking for 2-3 minutes.

2. Add Stock Gradually: Slowly add the stock while whisking continuously.

3. Simmer: Cook for 10-15 minutes until the sauce thickens to a smooth consistency. Season to taste.

Derivative Sauces:

- Supreme Sauce: Add cream and reduce for a richer sauce.

- Normande Sauce: Add mushroom stock and cream for use with seafood.

Uses in Modern Cooking:

- Chicken pot pie, poached fish, and light gravies.

3. Espagnole: The Robust Base

Espagnole, or brown sauce, is a rich, flavorful sauce made with brown stock, tomato paste, and aromatics. It forms the basis of many hearty sauces like demi-glace.

Ingredients:

- 2 tablespoons butter

- 2 tablespoons flour

- 2 cups brown stock (beef or veal)

- 1 tablespoon tomato paste

- 1 small onion, diced

- 1 carrot, diced

- 1 celery stalk, diced

- Bay leaf and thyme

Instructions:

1. Make a Roux: Melt butter and stir in flour, cooking until the roux turns a light brown color.

2. Cook Vegetables: Add diced onion, carrot, and celery to the roux and cook until softened.

3. Add Stock and Tomato Paste: Stir in the stock and tomato paste. Add the bay leaf and thyme.

4. Simmer and Strain: Simmer for 30-40 minutes, then strain the sauce.

Derivative Sauces:

- Demi-Glace: Reduce Espagnole and brown stock together for an intensely rich sauce.

- Bordelaise: Add red wine, shallots, and bone marrow.

Uses in Modern Cooking:

- Beef bourguignon, braised short ribs, and meat gravies.

4. Hollandaise: Rich and Tangy

Hollandaise is an emulsion of butter, egg yolks, and lemon juice, known for its velvety texture and tangy flavor. It's a favorite for brunch dishes.

Ingredients:

- 3 egg yolks

- 1/2 cup clarified butter (warm)

- 1 tablespoon lemon juice

- Salt and cayenne pepper

Instructions:

1. Whisk Egg Yolks: Place egg yolks and lemon juice in a heatproof bowl. Whisk until thickened.

2. Cook Over Gentle Heat: Place the bowl over simmering water (double boiler) and whisk continuously.

3. Add Butter Gradually: Slowly drizzle in the clarified butter while whisking.

4. Season: Add salt and cayenne pepper to taste.

Derivative Sauces:

- Béarnaise Sauce: Add tarragon and shallots for a fragrant variation.

- Mousseline Sauce: Fold in whipped cream for an airy texture.

Uses in Modern Cooking:

- Eggs Benedict, steamed asparagus, grilled salmon, and roasted vegetables.

5. Tomato Sauce: A Universal Favorite

Tomato sauce is perhaps the most universally recognized mother sauce, forming the base for countless Italian, Mediterranean, and global dishes.

Ingredients:

- 2 tablespoons olive oil

- 1 onion, finely diced

- 2 garlic cloves, minced
- 1 can (28 oz) crushed tomatoes
- 1 teaspoon sugar
- 1 teaspoon dried oregano or basil
- Salt and pepper

Instructions:

1. Sauté Aromatics: Heat olive oil in a saucepan and cook onion and garlic until softened.

2. Add Tomatoes and Seasonings: Stir in crushed tomatoes, sugar, oregano, salt, and pepper.

3. Simmer: Cook over low heat for 20-30 minutes, stirring occasionally.

Derivative Sauces:

- Marinara Sauce: Add fresh basil and extra garlic for a lighter variation.
- Arrabbiata Sauce: Add red chili flakes for a spicy kick.

Uses in Modern Cooking:

- Pasta dishes, pizza, ratatouille, and braised meats.

Variations and Uses in Modern Cooking

1. Adapting to Global Cuisines

While the mother sauces are rooted in French cuisine, they can be adapted to suit various culinary traditions:

- Béchamel in Greek Moussaka: Add cinnamon and nutmeg for Mediterranean flair.

- Tomato Sauce in Indian Curries: Use with added spices like cumin, coriander, and turmeric.

- Espagnole in Mexican Mole: Enhance with chocolate, chili, and cinnamon.

2. Modern Twists on Classic Sauces

Contemporary cooking often blends traditional techniques with modern ingredients:

- Vegan béchamel made with plant-based milk and butter.
- Hollandaise with avocado for a lighter, healthier option.

- Tomato sauce enhanced with roasted red peppers or sun-dried tomatoes.

Pro Tip: Experiment with fresh herbs, spices, and flavorings to make each sauce uniquely yours.

Closing Thoughts

Mastering the five mother sauces is a rite of passage for any aspiring cook, providing a foundation for culinary creativity. Whether you're crafting a comforting macaroni and cheese or an elegant bordelaise for a steak dinner, these sauces offer endless possibilities. As you practice and experiment, you'll discover new ways to adapt and innovate, keeping these classic sauces relevant in modern cooking. Let's continue the journey and elevate your sauce-making skills to new heights!

Chapter 2: The Science of Emulsions

Emulsions are among the most fascinating phenomena in the culinary world, where seemingly incompatible ingredients like oil and water come together to create smooth, luscious textures and complex flavors. From a simple vinaigrette to rich hollandaise or creamy mayonnaise, emulsions are essential in elevating everyday dishes. But what makes them stable? Why do they sometimes break? And how can you fix them when they do?

In this chapter, we'll explore the science behind emulsions, walk through the process of creating three classic examples, and provide tips for troubleshooting and perfecting your emulsified creations.

What Makes Emulsions Stable?

1. What Is an Emulsion?

An emulsion is a mixture of two immiscible liquids, such as oil and water, that are forced to blend into a stable mixture. This is achieved by breaking one liquid into tiny droplets and dispersing them evenly throughout the other.

Types of Emulsions:

- Oil-in-Water Emulsions: Oil droplets are dispersed in water (e.g., vinaigrettes, hollandaise).

- Water-in-Oil Emulsions: Water droplets are dispersed in oil (e.g., butter, cream-based sauces).

2. The Role of Emulsifiers

An emulsifier is a substance that helps stabilize emulsions by reducing the surface tension between the oil and water.

Common Emulsifiers:

- Lecithin: Found in egg yolks and soy; essential for making mayonnaise and hollandaise.

- Mustard: Contains natural emulsifying properties, often used in vinaigrettes.

- Dairy Proteins: Cream and butter rely on casein proteins to stabilize water-in-oil emulsions.

Pro Tip: Always include an emulsifier when making emulsions to increase their stability and longevity.

3. Agitation: The Force Behind Emulsions

Agitation is crucial for forming emulsions, as it breaks one liquid into small droplets and disperses them into the other. Methods of agitation include:
- Whisking: Common for small batches of vinaigrettes or hollandaise.
- Blending: Ideal for smooth, creamy emulsions like mayonnaise.
- Shaking: Works well for vinaigrettes in a sealed jar.

Creating Classic Emulsions

1. Vinaigrettes: The Simple Emulsion

Vinaigrettes are the easiest emulsions to master and a staple for salads, marinades, and more.
Ingredients:
- 3 parts oil (olive oil, canola oil, etc.)
- 1 part acid (vinegar or citrus juice)
- 1 teaspoon mustard (optional, for stability)
- Salt and pepper to taste
Instructions:
1. Combine Ingredients: In a bowl, whisk together vinegar, mustard, salt, and pepper.
2. Add Oil Gradually: Slowly drizzle in the oil while whisking continuously.
3. Emulsify: Continue whisking until the mixture thickens and becomes smooth.
Tips for Success:
- Use a 3:1 oil-to-acid ratio as a guideline, but adjust to taste.
- For added flavor, incorporate herbs, garlic, or honey.

2. Mayonnaise: The Creamy Emulsion

Mayonnaise is a stable emulsion that combines oil and egg yolks for a rich, creamy texture.

Ingredients:

- 2 egg yolks

- 1 cup neutral oil (canola or vegetable oil)

- 1 tablespoon vinegar or lemon juice

- 1 teaspoon Dijon mustard

- Salt to taste

Instructions:

1. Prepare the Base: In a bowl, whisk egg yolks, mustard, and vinegar until smooth.

2. Add Oil Slowly: Begin adding oil drop by drop while whisking continuously. Once the mixture thickens, add the oil in a slow stream.

3. Season: Whisk in salt and adjust the acidity with more lemon juice or vinegar if needed.

Pro Tip: Use a blender or food processor for a faster, more stable emulsion.

3. Hollandaise: The Velvety Emulsion

Hollandaise is a warm emulsion made with egg yolks and clarified butter, known for its silky texture and tangy flavor.

Ingredients:

- 3 egg yolks

- 1/2 cup clarified butter (warm)

- 1 tablespoon lemon juice

- Pinch of cayenne pepper

- Salt to taste

Instructions:

1. Whisk Egg Yolks: In a heatproof bowl, whisk egg yolks and lemon juice until thickened.

2. Set Up Double Boiler: Place the bowl over simmering water, ensuring it doesn't touch the water. Whisk continuously.

3. Add Butter: Gradually drizzle in warm clarified butter while whisking until the sauce thickens.

4. Season: Add cayenne pepper and salt to taste.

Pro Tip: Maintain low heat to prevent the eggs from scrambling.

Troubleshooting Common Issues

1. Emulsion Breaking

An emulsion is said to "break" when the oil and water separate, resulting in a curdled or split texture.

Causes of Breaking:

- Adding oil too quickly.

- Using too much oil relative to the emulsifier.

- Overheating (especially in hollandaise).

- Insufficient whisking or agitation.

2. Fixing a Broken Emulsion

1. Vinaigrettes:

- Whisk vigorously to re-emulsify or add a small amount of mustard for stability.

2. Mayonnaise:

- Start a new emulsion with one egg yolk, then slowly whisk in the broken mixture.

3. Hollandaise:

- Remove from heat and whisk in a teaspoon of warm water to bring it back together.

Pro Tip: Prevent breaking by adding oil slowly and maintaining consistent whisking.

3. Grainy or Lumpy Texture

Causes:

- Improper mixing or uneven heat distribution.

Fix:
- Strain the mixture through a fine-mesh sieve to remove lumps.

4. Separation After Resting

Emulsions naturally separate over time, especially vinaigrettes. To remedy this:
- Shake or whisk the mixture again before use.
- For long-term storage, add a stabilizer like mustard or xanthan gum.

Advanced Tips for Perfect Emulsions

1. Use Room-Temperature Ingredients

Cold ingredients can inhibit emulsification. Allow eggs, butter, and oil to come to room temperature before starting.

2. Choose the Right Tools

A whisk works well for small batches, while a blender or immersion blender ensures stability for larger quantities.

3. Experiment with Ratios and Flavors

Adjust oil-to-liquid ratios to create emulsions of varying thicknesses. Incorporate flavorings like garlic, herbs, or spices for unique variations.

Modern Applications of Emulsions

- Salad Dressings: Beyond vinaigrettes, emulsions like tahini dressing or creamy avocado dressings elevate greens.
- Dipping Sauces: Aioli and remoulade add depth to fried or grilled dishes.
- Sauces for Proteins: Hollandaise pairs beautifully with eggs, asparagus, or fish.
- Desserts: Emulsions like chocolate ganache rely on similar principles.

Closing Thoughts

Mastering emulsions is a gateway to creating dishes with luxurious textures and balanced flavors. By understanding the science behind them, perfecting techniques, and troubleshooting issues, you'll gain the confidence to tackle everything from simple vinaigrettes to complex hollandaise. Emulsions are more than just culinary science—they're an art form, and with practice, they can become your most versatile tool in the kitchen. Let's move forward to explore even more ways to elevate your cooking!

Chapter 3: Essential Pantry Sauces

Sauces are the unsung heroes of any meal, capable of transforming a simple dish into a culinary masterpiece. While the classics like béchamel and hollandaise require specific techniques, there's a world of quick and versatile sauces that can be whipped up using pantry staples. These essential sauces are not just time-savers; they're flavor boosters that every home cook should have in their repertoire.

In this chapter, we'll explore the building blocks of pantry sauces, walk through step-by-step recipes for soy glaze, garlic butter sauce, and honey mustard dressing, and offer tips for improvising with what's on hand to create endless variations.

Building Blocks for Quick and Versatile Sauces

1. Understanding Pantry Staples

Creating a great sauce doesn't require a trip to the grocery store. With a well-stocked pantry, you can build a wide range of sauces that suit almost any dish. The key is understanding how to combine staple ingredients into cohesive flavors.

Essential Pantry Ingredients for Sauces:

1. Oils and Fats: Olive oil, vegetable oil, sesame oil, and butter are the base of many sauces.

2. Acids: Vinegars (balsamic, red wine, rice, and apple cider) and citrus juices (lemon, lime).

3. Sweeteners: Sugar, honey, maple syrup, and molasses add balance and complexity.

4. Salty Elements: Soy sauce, miso paste, fish sauce, and salt provide umami and seasoning.

5. Aromatics: Garlic, onions, shallots, and ginger infuse sauces with depth.

6. Spices and Herbs: Black pepper, chili flakes, cumin, paprika, and fresh or dried herbs.

7. Thickeners: Cornstarch, flour, and cream help achieve the desired consistency.

Pro Tip: Organize your pantry so these staples are always accessible, and restock regularly to maintain freshness.

2. The Anatomy of a Sauce

A well-balanced sauce relies on a combination of key elements:
- Base: Provides body and richness (e.g., oil, butter, or cream).
- Flavor Enhancers: Add complexity, such as soy sauce, mustard, or vinegar.
- Thickener: Gives the sauce the right texture, such as cornstarch or a roux.
- Seasonings: Adjust the final flavor with salt, pepper, or fresh herbs.

Pro Tip: Taste as you go. Start with small amounts of seasoning and adjust to your liking.

3. Techniques for Quick Sauces

Many pantry sauces can be prepared in minutes with simple methods:
- Reduction: Simmer liquid ingredients to concentrate their flavors and thicken the sauce.
- Emulsification: Whisk oil into an acidic base (vinegar or citrus) for creamy dressings.
- Sautéing: Cook aromatics like garlic or onion in oil or butter to infuse the base with flavor.
- Blending: Use an immersion blender to quickly combine ingredients into a smooth sauce.

Recipes: Quick and Versatile Pantry Sauces

1. Soy Glaze

A soy glaze is a rich, umami-packed sauce that's perfect for drizzling over roasted vegetables, grilled meats, or even rice bowls.

Ingredients:
- 1/2 cup soy sauce
- 1/4 cup honey or maple syrup

- 1 tablespoon rice vinegar

- 1 teaspoon sesame oil

- 1 teaspoon minced garlic

- 1 teaspoon minced ginger

- 1 teaspoon cornstarch (optional, for thickening)

Instructions:

1. Combine Ingredients: In a small saucepan, mix soy sauce, honey, rice vinegar, sesame oil, garlic, and ginger.

2. Simmer: Heat over medium heat, stirring occasionally, until the mixture begins to reduce and thicken (5-7 minutes).

3. Thicken (Optional): For a thicker glaze, mix cornstarch with 1 tablespoon of water and stir into the sauce. Cook for an additional 2 minutes.

4. Cool and Store: Let the glaze cool slightly before using. Store leftovers in an airtight container in the refrigerator for up to a week.

Pro Tip: Add a pinch of chili flakes for a spicy kick.

2. Garlic Butter Sauce

Garlic butter sauce is a versatile favorite, ideal for pasta, seafood, vegetables, or dipping bread.

Ingredients:

- 4 tablespoons unsalted butter

- 4 garlic cloves, minced

- 1 tablespoon lemon juice

- 1/4 teaspoon salt

- 2 tablespoons chopped parsley (optional)

Instructions:

1. Melt Butter: In a small skillet or saucepan, melt butter over medium heat.

2. Cook Garlic: Add minced garlic and sauté for 1-2 minutes, stirring frequently, until fragrant (do not let it brown).

3. Add Lemon Juice: Stir in lemon juice and salt, then cook for another 1 minute.

4. Garnish: Remove from heat and stir in chopped parsley if desired.

Pro Tip: For extra richness, add a splash of heavy cream or grated Parmesan cheese.

3. Honey Mustard Dressing

Honey mustard dressing strikes the perfect balance between tangy and sweet, making it ideal for salads, sandwiches, or as a dipping sauce.

Ingredients:

- 1/4 cup Dijon mustard

- 1/4 cup honey

- 2 tablespoons apple cider vinegar

- 1/4 cup olive oil

- Salt and pepper to taste

Instructions:

1. Mix Base Ingredients: In a bowl, whisk together Dijon mustard, honey, and vinegar until smooth.

2. Add Oil Gradually: Slowly drizzle in olive oil while whisking continuously to create an emulsion.

3. Season: Adjust with salt and pepper to taste.

Pro Tip: Add a pinch of cayenne for heat or fresh herbs like dill for added flavor.

Tips for Improvising with What's on Hand

1. Substitute Ingredients

Running out of an ingredient doesn't mean you can't make a great sauce. Substitute with what you have on hand:

- Soy Sauce: Replace with tamari or coconut aminos for a gluten-free option.

- Honey: Swap with maple syrup, agave nectar, or brown sugar.

- Vinegar: Use lemon juice, lime juice, or another type of vinegar.

Pro Tip: Keep a list of substitutes handy to experiment confidently.

2. Adjust Flavor Profiles

Modify your sauces to suit different cuisines or preferences:

- Add Heat: Include chili flakes, sriracha, or hot sauce for spice.

- Boost Umami: Incorporate miso, anchovy paste, or Parmesan.

- Brighten with Acidity: Finish with a splash of citrus juice or vinegar.

Pro Tip: If your sauce is too salty, balance it with a touch of sweetness or acidity.

3. Experiment with Textures

Don't be afraid to adjust the consistency of your sauce:

- Thicken: Use cornstarch, flour, or pureed vegetables.

- Thin: Add water, broth, or milk.

Pro Tip: For a creamy texture, blend in avocado, yogurt, or tahini.

Versatility of Pantry Sauces

1. Multipurpose Applications

These sauces aren't limited to a single use:

- Soy Glaze: Drizzle over roasted veggies, use as a marinade, or glaze chicken thighs.

- Garlic Butter Sauce: Toss with pasta, pour over shrimp, or serve with crusty bread.

- Honey Mustard Dressing: Use as a salad dressing, sandwich spread, or dipping sauce for chicken tenders.

2. Making Ahead

Most pantry sauces can be made ahead and stored for future use.

- Refrigeration: Store sauces in airtight containers in the fridge for 3-7 days.

- Freezing: Freeze in small portions using ice cube trays for easy use.

Pro Tip: Label containers with the date and ingredients to keep track of freshness.

Closing Thoughts

Mastering pantry sauces is an essential skill for any cook, offering endless opportunities to create flavorful dishes with minimal effort. By understanding the basic building blocks, experimenting with substitutions, and learning key techniques, you can craft quick, versatile sauces that elevate your meals. Whether it's a rich garlic butter sauce, a tangy honey mustard dressing, or a bold soy glaze, these recipes are just the beginning. Let's continue exploring the art of sauce-making to unlock even more delicious possibilities!

Chapter 4: Creamy Sauces for Comfort Foods

Creamy sauces are the epitome of comfort, adding richness and indulgence to dishes ranging from pasta and casseroles to roasted vegetables. A velvety Alfredo sauce poured over fettuccine, a gooey cheese sauce smothering baked potatoes, or a delicate mushroom cream sauce draped over roasted chicken—these sauces elevate everyday meals into decadent delights.

This chapter delves into the art of creating rich and creamy sauces, explores the importance of balancing richness with acidity, and provides step-by-step recipes for three beloved classics: Alfredo, cheese sauce, and mushroom cream sauce.

Mastering Rich and Creamy Sauces

1. The Science of Creamy Sauces

Creamy sauces rely on a combination of fat, liquid, and thickeners to achieve their signature texture. Understanding the role of each component is key to mastering them.

Key Ingredients in Creamy Sauces:

- Fats: Butter, cream, cheese, and oils form the foundation.
- Liquids: Milk, cream, or stock provide volume and lighten the sauce.
- Thickeners: Flour, cornstarch, or egg yolks stabilize and thicken.
- Seasonings: Salt, pepper, and aromatics like garlic, shallots, and herbs enhance flavor.

Pro Tip: Use high-quality ingredients to ensure a smooth, rich, and flavorful sauce.

2. Techniques for Perfect Creaminess

Achieving a creamy texture involves precise techniques that prevent curdling, clumping, or separation.

Essential Techniques:

1. Low and Slow Heat: Gentle heat prevents scorching or curdling.

2. Constant Stirring: Keeps ingredients evenly distributed and prevents sticking.

3. Incorporate Gradually: Add liquids slowly to avoid lumps, especially when using a roux.

4. Balance Flavors: Use acidic elements (lemon juice, wine, or vinegar) sparingly to cut through richness without overpowering.

Pro Tip: Always taste and adjust seasoning as you cook.

3. Balancing Richness with Acidity

Creamy sauces can feel heavy if not balanced properly. Acidity brightens the flavors, making the sauce more palatable.

Balancing Elements:

- Wine: A splash of white wine adds depth and tang to Alfredo or mushroom sauces.

- Citrus: Lemon juice pairs beautifully with cheese or butter-based sauces.

- Vinegar: A touch of balsamic or apple cider vinegar can elevate creamy dressings.

Pro Tip: Add acidic components at the end of cooking to preserve their brightness.

Recipes: Classic Creamy Sauces

1. Alfredo Sauce

Alfredo sauce is a classic Italian-American staple known for its luxurious creaminess and subtle garlic flavor. Perfect for pasta or drizzling over roasted vegetables.

Ingredients:

- 1/2 cup unsalted butter
- 2 cups heavy cream
- 2 garlic cloves, minced
- 1 cup freshly grated Parmesan cheese
- Salt and black pepper to taste
- Fresh parsley (optional, for garnish)

Instructions:

1. Melt Butter: In a large saucepan, melt butter over medium heat. Add minced garlic and sauté until fragrant (1-2 minutes).

2. Add Cream: Pour in heavy cream and bring to a gentle simmer. Stir frequently.

3. Incorporate Cheese: Gradually whisk in Parmesan cheese until melted and smooth.

4. Season: Add salt and black pepper to taste. Simmer for another 2-3 minutes.

5. Serve: Toss with fettuccine or drizzle over roasted vegetables. Garnish with parsley if desired.

Pro Tip: For a lighter version, substitute half-and-half for heavy cream.

2. Cheese Sauce

Cheese sauce is a versatile favorite, perfect for mac and cheese, nachos, or as a dip for vegetables.

Ingredients:

- 2 tablespoons butter
- 2 tablespoons all-purpose flour
- 2 cups milk
- 2 cups shredded sharp cheddar cheese
- 1/2 teaspoon Dijon mustard
- Salt and cayenne pepper to taste

Instructions:

1. Make a Roux: In a saucepan, melt butter over medium heat. Stir in flour and cook for 1-2 minutes, whisking constantly.

2. Add Milk Gradually: Slowly pour in milk, whisking to combine. Cook until the mixture thickens (3-5 minutes).

3. Melt Cheese: Reduce heat to low and stir in shredded cheese until fully melted and smooth.

4. Season: Add Dijon mustard, salt, and a pinch of cayenne pepper. Adjust seasoning to taste.

5. Serve: Pour over steamed broccoli, baked potatoes, or pasta.

Pro Tip: For a smoother sauce, use freshly grated cheese rather than pre-shredded, which often contains anti-caking agents.

3. Mushroom Cream Sauce

Mushroom cream sauce is earthy and indulgent, ideal for steak, chicken, or as a topping for mashed potatoes.

Ingredients:

- 2 tablespoons olive oil
- 1 tablespoon butter
- 1 pound mushrooms (button or cremini), sliced
- 2 garlic cloves, minced
- 1/2 cup dry white wine
- 1 cup heavy cream
- 1 teaspoon thyme (fresh or dried)
- Salt and black pepper to taste

Instructions:

1. Cook Mushrooms: Heat olive oil and butter in a skillet over medium heat. Add mushrooms and cook until golden brown (5-7 minutes).

2. Add Garlic: Stir in minced garlic and cook for 1 minute.

3. Deglaze with Wine: Pour in white wine, scraping up browned bits from the skillet. Simmer until the wine reduces by half.

4. Add Cream and Thyme: Stir in heavy cream and thyme. Simmer for 3-5 minutes until thickened.

5. Season: Add salt and black pepper to taste. Serve immediately.

Pro Tip: For added depth, mix in a teaspoon of Dijon mustard or a splash of Worcestershire sauce.

Pairing Creamy Sauces with Dishes

1. Pastas

Creamy sauces are a natural match for pasta, coating each strand or piece beautifully.

- Alfredo pairs well with fettuccine, tortellini, or ravioli.
- Cheese sauce transforms elbow macaroni into a childhood classic.

Pro Tip: Reserve some pasta water to loosen sauces if they become too thick.

2. Vegetables

Creamy sauces can make even the simplest vegetables indulgent:
- Drizzle cheese sauce over steamed broccoli or cauliflower.
- Toss roasted Brussels sprouts in Alfredo for a unique twist.

Pro Tip: Add a pinch of nutmeg to cream-based sauces for a subtle warmth that complements vegetables.

3. Proteins

Rich sauces enhance the flavor of proteins:
- Pair mushroom cream sauce with seared chicken thighs or grilled steak.
- Use cheese sauce as a topping for baked chicken breasts or turkey meatloaf.

Pro Tip: Finish protein-based dishes with fresh herbs or a squeeze of lemon for brightness.

Tips for Perfect Creamy Sauces

1. Avoid Overheating

High heat can cause cream or cheese to curdle. Keep the heat low and stir continuously.

2. Use Fresh Ingredients

Fresh cream, butter, and cheese yield the best flavor and texture.

3. Customize Flavors

Experiment with different cheeses, herbs, and spices to create unique variations of classic sauces.

Closing Thoughts

Mastering creamy sauces is a gateway to crafting rich, comforting meals that satisfy the soul. Whether it's the indulgence of Alfredo, the gooey goodness of cheese sauce, or the earthy depth of mushroom cream sauce, these recipes are versatile and easy to adapt to your preferences. By balancing richness with acidity and using quality ingredients, you'll be able to elevate everyday dishes into something truly special. Let's continue exploring the world of sauces and discover even more ways to create culinary magic!

Chapter 5: Bold and Tangy Barbecue Sauces

Barbecue is more than a method of cooking; it's a culinary tradition steeped in history and culture. At the heart of every great barbecue experience is the sauce. From the sweet and smoky sauces of Kansas City to the tangy, mustard-based flavors of South Carolina and the fiery vinegar punches of Eastern Carolina, barbecue sauces are as diverse as the regions they hail from. Understanding these regional differences, mastering recipes, and knowing how to pair sauces with meats and grilling techniques can take your barbecue skills to the next level.

This chapter explores the vibrant world of barbecue sauces, delves into their regional nuances, provides step-by-step recipes for three classic styles, and offers tips for pairing sauces with meats and perfecting grilling techniques.

Regional Differences in Barbecue Sauces

Barbecue sauce is as much about tradition as it is about taste. Each region in the United States has developed its signature style, reflecting local ingredients, cooking methods, and cultural influences.

1. Kansas City Style: Sweet and Smoky

Kansas City barbecue sauce is perhaps the most widely recognized style. Thick, rich, and sweet with a smoky undertone, this sauce pairs beautifully with ribs, pulled pork, and chicken.

Key Characteristics:
- Sweet Base: Usually made with molasses or brown sugar.
- Tomato-Based: Typically uses ketchup or tomato paste.
- Smoky Flavor: Enhanced with liquid smoke or smoked paprika.

Pro Tip: Kansas City sauces are ideal for glazing meats during the last stages of grilling.

2. Carolina Style: Tangy and Diverse

Carolina barbecue sauces vary significantly by region, with three main styles:
- Eastern Carolina: Vinegar-based and thin, with no tomato.

- Western Carolina (Lexington): Adds a touch of ketchup for sweetness.
- South Carolina: Mustard-based with a tangy, slightly sweet profile.
Key Characteristics:
- Vinegar and mustard are the stars.
- Light and tangy, designed to cut through the richness of pork.
- Often used as a mop sauce during cooking.
Pro Tip: Carolina sauces pair perfectly with pulled pork or whole hog barbecue.

3. Texas Style: Bold and Savory

Texas barbecue is all about the meat, and the sauces are typically bold, thin, and peppery, designed to complement rather than overpower.
Key Characteristics:
- Simplicity: Often beef stock-based with minimal sugar.
- Spice: Includes chili powder, black pepper, and cumin.
- Tomato-Based: Uses tomato paste or sauce sparingly.
Pro Tip: Use Texas-style sauces as a basting liquid for brisket or beef ribs.

4. Memphis Style: Balanced and Complex

Memphis barbecue sauce strikes a balance between sweet, tangy, and spicy. It's thinner than Kansas City sauces but richer than Carolina styles.
Key Characteristics:
- A mix of tomato, vinegar, and molasses.
- Spices like garlic, onion powder, and cayenne add depth.
- Often served as a side sauce rather than slathered on during cooking.
Pro Tip: Memphis sauces work well as a finishing sauce for dry-rubbed ribs.

Recipes: Classic Barbecue Sauces

1. Sweet and Smoky Barbecue Sauce (Kansas City Style)

This rich, sticky sauce is a crowd-pleaser, perfect for glazing ribs or slathering on burgers.
Ingredients:

- 1 cup ketchup
- 1/4 cup molasses
- 1/4 cup brown sugar
- 2 tablespoons apple cider vinegar
- 1 tablespoon Worcestershire sauce
- 1 teaspoon smoked paprika
- 1/2 teaspoon garlic powder
- 1/2 teaspoon onion powder
- 1/4 teaspoon cayenne pepper (optional)
- Salt and black pepper to taste

Instructions:

1. Combine Ingredients: In a saucepan, mix all ingredients.

2. Simmer: Heat over medium heat until the sauce begins to bubble. Reduce heat to low and simmer for 10-15 minutes, stirring occasionally.

3. Adjust Seasoning: Taste and adjust sweetness, tanginess, or heat as desired.

4. Cool and Store: Let the sauce cool before transferring to a jar. Store in the refrigerator for up to two weeks.

Pro Tip: Brush this sauce onto ribs during the last 10 minutes of grilling for a caramelized glaze.

2. Mustard-Based Barbecue Sauce (South Carolina Style)

Tangy and slightly sweet, this mustard-based sauce is a unique addition to your barbecue repertoire.

Ingredients:

- 1/2 cup yellow mustard
- 1/4 cup apple cider vinegar
- 2 tablespoons honey or brown sugar
- 1 tablespoon Worcestershire sauce
- 1 teaspoon garlic powder
- 1/2 teaspoon smoked paprika
- 1/4 teaspoon cayenne pepper (optional)
- Salt and black pepper to taste

Instructions:

1. Mix Ingredients: Combine all ingredients in a small saucepan.

2. Heat Gently: Warm over low heat, stirring frequently, until the sugar dissolves and the flavors meld (5-7 minutes).

3. Cool and Serve: Let cool before serving with pulled pork or grilled chicken.

Pro Tip: This sauce doubles as a marinade for pork or chicken.

3. Spicy Vinegar Sauce (Eastern Carolina Style)

This thin, fiery sauce cuts through the richness of smoked pork with its bold vinegar base.

Ingredients:

- 1 cup apple cider vinegar
- 1/4 cup white vinegar
- 1 tablespoon sugar
- 1 tablespoon red pepper flakes
- 1 teaspoon black pepper
- 1/2 teaspoon salt

Instructions:

1. Combine Ingredients: Mix all ingredients in a jar or bowl.

2. Infuse Flavors: Let sit at room temperature for at least an hour to allow the flavors to meld.

3. Serve: Use as a mop sauce during cooking or drizzle over pulled pork before serving.

Pro Tip: Store this sauce in a sealed jar in the refrigerator for up to a month.

Pairing Sauces with Meats and Grilling Techniques

1. Pairing Barbecue Sauces with Meats

The right sauce can elevate the natural flavors of meat. Here's a guide to pairing:

- Ribs: Sweet and smoky sauces caramelize beautifully, creating a sticky glaze.

- Pulled Pork: Tangy vinegar or mustard-based sauces balance the richness.

- Brisket: Bold, peppery Texas-style sauces enhance the smoky flavors.

- Chicken: Versatile; pairs well with sweet, tangy, or spicy sauces.

Pro Tip: Always let the meat shine—use sauces to complement, not mask, its flavor.

2. Grilling Techniques for Perfect Sauces

1. Timing Is Everything:
   - Apply sauces during the last 10-15 minutes of grilling to prevent burning.
   2. Use Indirect Heat:
   - Keep sauced meats on the cooler side of the grill to avoid scorching.
   3. Basting:
   - Use a silicone brush or mop to apply thin layers of sauce, building up flavor gradually.

Pro Tip: Reserve some sauce for serving to add a fresh layer of flavor at the table.

Tips for Customizing Barbecue Sauces

1. Adjust Sweetness: Add more molasses or honey for a sweeter profile.

2. Boost Heat: Incorporate cayenne, chili powder, or hot sauce for a fiery kick.

3. Experiment with Acidity: Swap vinegar types or add citrus juice for a tangy twist.

4. Infuse Smoke: Add a few drops of liquid smoke for that outdoor barbecue flavor.

Pro Tip: Keep tasting as you cook to balance flavors perfectly.

Closing Thoughts

Bold and tangy barbecue sauces are an essential part of creating unforgettable grilling experiences. By mastering regional styles and learning how to pair sauces with meats and techniques, you'll be ready to impress at your next cookout. Whether you're crafting a sweet and smoky Kansas City sauce, a tangy mustard-based South Carolina sauce, or a fiery Eastern Carolina vinegar sauce, each recipe adds a unique flavor that complements your grilling expertise.

Let's keep exploring the world of sauces and take your barbecue game to new heights!

Chapter 6: Bright and Herby Green Sauces

Herb-based green sauces are among the most versatile and vibrant additions to any dish. They bring freshness, color, and a burst of flavor to grilled meats, roasted vegetables, and even pasta. Rooted in various culinary traditions, these sauces—like chimichurri from Argentina, pesto from Italy, and salsa verde from Mexico or Spain—celebrate the natural beauty of fresh herbs and greens.

In this chapter, we'll explore the magic of bright and herby green sauces, provide recipes for three iconic variations, and teach you how to customize these sauces using seasonal ingredients and your personal creativity.

Why Green Sauces?

1. A Burst of Freshness

Green sauces are like a breath of fresh air for your palate. They cut through the richness of heavy dishes and enhance lighter ones with their tangy, herby profiles.

Key Benefits:
- Freshness: Their vibrant flavors balance rich and savory meals.
- Versatility: Perfect as marinades, dips, spreads, or toppings.
- Nutritional Boost: Packed with vitamins and antioxidants from fresh herbs and greens.

Pro Tip: Use green sauces to elevate even the simplest dishes, like grilled chicken or steamed vegetables.

2. The Global Appeal of Green Sauces

Every culture has its version of a green sauce, each offering a unique twist based on local ingredients and traditions.

- Chimichurri (Argentina): A tangy, garlic-forward sauce made with parsley, oregano, and olive oil.
- Pesto (Italy): A creamy blend of basil, pine nuts, Parmesan, and olive oil.

- Salsa Verde (Mexico/Spain): A zesty sauce made with tomatillos or parsley, often spiked with lime or vinegar.

Pro Tip: Experiment with these sauces as bases to create your own signature versions.

The Anatomy of a Perfect Green Sauce

Green sauces typically consist of a balance of the following components:

1. Herbs or Greens: The foundation of the sauce, providing vibrant color and flavor. Examples include basil, parsley, cilantro, spinach, or arugula.

2. Oil or Fat: Olive oil or other neutral oils emulsify the sauce and add richness.

3. Acid: Lemon juice, lime juice, or vinegar brightens and balances the flavors.

4. Aromatics: Garlic, shallots, or onions bring depth.

5. Seasoning: Salt, pepper, and spices enhance the overall profile.

6. Optional Add-Ins: Nuts, cheese, or chili peppers add texture and flavor complexity.

Pro Tip: Taste as you go, adjusting each component to suit your dish and preferences.

Recipes: Bright and Herby Green Sauces

1. Chimichurri

This bold and tangy Argentinian sauce is a staple for grilled meats, especially steak, but it's just as delicious on roasted vegetables or as a bread dip.

Ingredients:
- 1 cup fresh parsley leaves, finely chopped
- 1/4 cup fresh oregano leaves, finely chopped
- 3 garlic cloves, minced
- 1/4 cup red wine vinegar
- 1/2 cup olive oil
- 1 teaspoon red chili flakes

- Salt and black pepper to taste

Instructions:

1. Combine Herbs and Garlic: In a bowl, mix parsley, oregano, and garlic.

2. Add Acid and Oil: Stir in red wine vinegar and olive oil. Mix well.

3. Season: Add red chili flakes, salt, and black pepper to taste. Adjust the acid or oil as needed.

4. Serve: Use immediately or store in the refrigerator for up to one week.

Pro Tip: For a smoother consistency, pulse the ingredients in a food processor.

2. Pesto

Pesto is an iconic Italian sauce known for its creamy texture and fragrant basil flavor. It's traditionally served with pasta but also works as a spread or dip.

Ingredients:

- 2 cups fresh basil leaves
- 1/4 cup pine nuts
- 2 garlic cloves
- 1/2 cup grated Parmesan cheese
- 1/2 cup olive oil
- Salt and black pepper to taste

Instructions:

1. Blend Ingredients: In a food processor, combine basil, pine nuts, garlic, and Parmesan. Pulse until coarsely chopped.

2. Add Oil Gradually: With the processor running, slowly drizzle in olive oil until the mixture reaches your desired consistency.

3. Season: Add salt and pepper to taste. Adjust oil if needed for a creamier texture.

4. Store: Refrigerate in an airtight container for up to a week, or freeze in ice cube trays for later use.

Pro Tip: Substitute walnuts or almonds for pine nuts to save on cost without sacrificing flavor.

3. Salsa Verde

This zesty sauce has variations across cuisines, but the Mexican version features bright, tangy flavors perfect for tacos, grilled chicken, or seafood.

Ingredients:

- 8-10 tomatillos, husked and rinsed
- 1/2 cup fresh cilantro leaves
- 1 small onion, chopped
- 1 garlic clove
- 1 jalapeño or serrano pepper (adjust for heat)
- 1 tablespoon lime juice
- Salt to taste

Instructions:

1. Cook Tomatillos: Boil or roast tomatillos until softened and slightly charred.

2. Blend Ingredients: In a blender, combine cooked tomatillos, cilantro, onion, garlic, pepper, and lime juice. Blend until smooth.

3. Season: Add salt to taste. Adjust lime juice or pepper for brightness or heat.

4. Serve: Use immediately or refrigerate for up to five days.

Pro Tip: For a smoky twist, char the tomatillos and peppers over an open flame before blending.

How to Customize Herb Sauces with Seasonal Ingredients

1. Substituting Herbs and Greens

Green sauces are incredibly adaptable, allowing you to swap or mix herbs and greens based on seasonality or preference.

Spring: Use tender greens like arugula, spinach, or pea shoots.

Summer: Basil, cilantro, or mint thrive in the summer heat.

Fall: Parsley, sage, and kale offer heartier flavors.

Winter: Use frozen herbs or hardy greens like Swiss chard or collards.

Pro Tip: Combine different herbs for a more complex flavor profile (e.g., parsley and mint).

2. Adding Nuts and Seeds

Nuts and seeds add richness and texture to green sauces. Experiment with:
- Walnuts: Great for pestos and chimichurri.
- Sunflower Seeds: A budget-friendly alternative to pine nuts.
- Pistachios: Add sweetness and a vibrant green color.

Pro Tip: Toast nuts or seeds lightly before blending to enhance their flavor.

3. Experimenting with Acidity

The right acidity brightens green sauces. Customize with:
- Citrus: Lime for salsa verde, lemon for pesto.
- Vinegars: Red wine vinegar for chimichurri, apple cider vinegar for unique pestos.

Pro Tip: Add acidity in small amounts, tasting as you go to prevent overpowering the sauce.

4. Enhancing with Aromatics

Garlic, shallots, or scallions can transform a simple green sauce. Adjust the amount based on your taste preferences:
- Raw Garlic: Provides a sharp, pungent flavor.
- Roasted Garlic: Adds a milder, sweeter undertone.
- Shallots or Onions: Soften the bite of raw garlic in herb-based sauces.

Pro Tip: Sauté or roast aromatics for a more mellow flavor.

Pairing Green Sauces with Dishes

1. Proteins

- Grilled Meats: Chimichurri pairs perfectly with steak, chicken, or lamb.
- Seafood: Salsa verde adds brightness to grilled fish or shrimp.
- Eggs: Pesto drizzled over scrambled eggs or frittatas makes for a gourmet breakfast.

2. Vegetables

- Roasted Vegetables: Toss potatoes, carrots, or zucchini with chimichurri or pesto.

  - Salads: Use salsa verde as a tangy dressing for fresh greens or grain salads.

3. Bread and Pasta

- Bread Dipping: Serve pesto or chimichurri with warm crusty bread as an appetizer.

  - Pasta: Toss spaghetti or penne with pesto for a quick and satisfying meal.

  Pro Tip: Keep a jar of green sauce on hand to add instant flavor to any dish.

Closing Thoughts

Bright and herby green sauces bring vitality to your cooking, transforming simple ingredients into flavorful dishes. By mastering recipes like chimichurri, pesto, and salsa verde, and learning how to customize them with seasonal ingredients, you'll unlock endless possibilities in the kitchen. These sauces are not only a testament to the beauty of fresh herbs and greens but also a celebration of culinary creativity. Let's keep exploring new ways to enhance our meals with these vibrant, versatile sauces!

Chapter 7: Asian-Inspired Sauces

The diverse world of Asian sauces offers a symphony of flavors, blending sweet, salty, sour, spicy, and umami into versatile condiments and dressings. From the tangy brightness of a soy-ginger glaze to the nutty richness of Thai peanut sauce and the fiery depth of Korean gochujang, these sauces are essential tools in any cook's repertoire.

This chapter delves into the art and science of crafting Asian-inspired sauces, explores the key ingredients that define them, and provides step-by-step recipes for three iconic sauces. By understanding their flavor profiles and techniques, you'll be able to recreate authentic tastes or innovate with your own spin.

The Importance of Sauces in Asian Cuisine

1. A Foundation of Flavor

In Asian cooking, sauces are more than condiments—they're the foundation of the dish. They serve to marinate, season, glaze, and balance flavors, ensuring every bite is layered with complexity.

Functions of Asian Sauces:

- Marinades: Tenderize and flavor proteins before cooking.

- Dipping Sauces: Enhance the flavors of dumplings, spring rolls, and fried snacks.

- Cooking Sauces: Form the base for stir-fries, curries, and noodle dishes.

Pro Tip: The balance of flavors in Asian sauces—sweet, salty, sour, spicy, and umami—is key to their universal appeal.

2. Regional Influences

The diversity of Asian sauces reflects the unique culinary traditions of each region:

- East Asia: Soy sauce, miso, and sesame oil dominate.

- Southeast Asia: Fish sauce, coconut milk, and tamarind add bold, tropical flavors.

- South Asia: Curry sauces and chutneys rely on fragrant spices and herbs.
- Korean Cuisine: Gochujang and doenjang deliver heat and umami with depth.

Pro Tip: Understanding the ingredients and techniques of each region allows you to create authentic dishes or cross-cultural fusions.

Key Ingredients in Asian Sauces

1. Miso

A fermented soybean paste, miso is a cornerstone of Japanese cooking.
- Flavor Profile: Salty and umami-rich with a slightly tangy undertone.
- Uses: Soups, marinades, dressings, and glazes.
- Types: White (mild), yellow (medium), and red (robust).

Pro Tip: Use miso sparingly—its concentrated flavor can easily overpower a dish.

2. Sesame Oil

Sesame oil is a fragrant oil pressed from toasted sesame seeds.
- Flavor Profile: Nutty, aromatic, and slightly smoky.
- Uses: Drizzle over stir-fries, noodle dishes, or salads for a finishing touch.

Pro Tip: Add sesame oil at the end of cooking to preserve its delicate aroma.

3. Fish Sauce

Fish sauce, made from fermented fish and salt, is a staple in Southeast Asian cuisines.
- Flavor Profile: Intensely salty and umami-packed with a briny tang.
- Uses: Key in pad Thai, Vietnamese pho, and Thai green papaya salad.

Pro Tip: Combine fish sauce with lime juice and sugar to balance its intensity.

4. Rice Vinegar

Rice vinegar is a mild vinegar made from fermented rice.

- Flavor Profile: Lightly acidic with a sweet undertone.

- Uses: Sushi rice, pickles, marinades, and dipping sauces.

Pro Tip: Mix rice vinegar with soy sauce and sesame oil for a quick, balanced dressing.

Recipes: Iconic Asian Sauces

1. Soy-Ginger Glaze

This glossy, tangy glaze is perfect for marinating salmon, glazing chicken, or drizzling over roasted vegetables.

Ingredients:

- 1/4 cup soy sauce

- 2 tablespoons honey or brown sugar

- 1 tablespoon rice vinegar

- 1 teaspoon sesame oil

- 1 teaspoon grated fresh ginger

- 1 garlic clove, minced

- 1 teaspoon cornstarch mixed with 1 tablespoon water

Instructions:

1. Combine Ingredients: In a small saucepan, mix soy sauce, honey, rice vinegar, sesame oil, ginger, and garlic.

2. Simmer: Heat over medium heat until the mixture begins to bubble.

3. Thicken: Stir in the cornstarch slurry and cook for 1-2 minutes until the glaze thickens.

4. Serve: Let cool slightly and use immediately or store in the refrigerator for up to a week.

Pro Tip: Add a pinch of chili flakes for heat or a splash of orange juice for citrusy brightness.

2. Thai Peanut Sauce

Creamy, nutty, and slightly spicy, Thai peanut sauce pairs beautifully with satay, spring rolls, or noodles.

Ingredients:

- 1/2 cup peanut butter (natural, unsweetened)

- 2 tablespoons soy sauce
- 1 tablespoon fish sauce
- 1 tablespoon lime juice
- 1 tablespoon brown sugar or honey
- 1 teaspoon red curry paste or sriracha (optional)
- 1/4 cup coconut milk or water

Instructions:

1. Mix Base Ingredients: In a bowl, whisk together peanut butter, soy sauce, fish sauce, lime juice, and sugar.

2. Adjust Consistency: Gradually whisk in coconut milk or water until the sauce reaches your desired thickness.

3. Season: Add red curry paste or sriracha for spice, adjusting to taste.

Pro Tip: Garnish with chopped peanuts and cilantro for added texture and freshness.

3. Korean Gochujang Sauce

This spicy, savory, and slightly sweet sauce is a staple in Korean cooking, ideal for bibimbap, fried chicken, or grilled meats.

Ingredients:

- 2 tablespoons gochujang (Korean chili paste)
- 1 tablespoon soy sauce
- 1 tablespoon rice vinegar
- 1 tablespoon sesame oil
- 1 tablespoon honey or brown sugar
- 1 garlic clove, minced

Instructions:

1. Combine Ingredients: In a bowl, mix gochujang, soy sauce, rice vinegar, sesame oil, honey, and garlic.

2. Blend: Stir until smooth and well combined.

3. Serve: Use as a dipping sauce, marinade, or glaze.

Pro Tip: Adjust the sweetness or spice level by tweaking the honey and gochujang proportions.

Pairing Asian Sauces with Dishes

1. Proteins

- Soy-Ginger Glaze: Perfect for salmon, tofu, or grilled chicken thighs.

- Thai Peanut Sauce: Pairs beautifully with chicken satay, shrimp, or roasted cauliflower.

- Gochujang Sauce: Adds bold flavor to pork belly, fried chicken, or grilled beef ribs.

2. Vegetables

- Soy-Ginger Glaze: Drizzle over roasted Brussels sprouts or green beans.

- Thai Peanut Sauce: Toss with steamed broccoli or sweet potatoes.

- Gochujang Sauce: Use as a topping for roasted carrots or eggplant.

3. Noodles and Rice

- Soy-Ginger Glaze: Stir into lo mein or fried rice for extra flavor.

- Thai Peanut Sauce: Toss with rice noodles or serve over jasmine rice.

- Gochujang Sauce: Mix into fried rice or bibimbap for a spicy kick.

Pro Tip: Keep cooked noodles or rice on hand to create quick, sauce-driven meals.

Customizing Asian Sauces

1. Adjusting Heat Levels

Add chili paste, sriracha, or fresh chilies for spice, or tone it down by adding coconut milk or sugar.

2. Experimenting with Sweetness

Use honey, brown sugar, or even fruit juice to balance the heat or saltiness.

3. Exploring New Aromatics

Incorporate shallots, scallions, or lemongrass for depth and freshness.

Closing Thoughts

Asian-inspired sauces bring vibrant flavors and endless possibilities to your cooking. Whether you're creating a tangy soy-ginger glaze, a creamy Thai peanut sauce, or a bold gochujang-based masterpiece, these sauces are your gateway to the rich culinary traditions of Asia. By mastering the recipes and understanding the key ingredients, you can recreate authentic tastes or put your own creative spin on these classics. Let's keep exploring the world of sauces and uncover even more ways to elevate your dishes!

Chapter 8: Classic Gravy and Pan Sauces

Gravy and pan sauces are the ultimate finishing touches, elevating hearty meals with richness and depth. Whether drizzled over a succulent roast, poured on creamy mashed potatoes, or served alongside roasted vegetables, these sauces transform a meal into a luxurious dining experience. At their core, gravies and pan sauces are simple yet versatile, requiring only a few ingredients and a touch of technique to master.

This chapter explores the art of making gravy from drippings, provides step-by-step recipes for beef au jus, turkey gravy, and red wine reduction, and offers essential tips for achieving smooth, lump-free consistency.

The Art of Making Gravy from Drippings

1. Why Drippings Matter

Drippings are the flavorful juices, fat, and caramelized bits left behind after roasting meat. These golden remnants are the foundation of a great gravy, carrying the essence of the roast into the sauce.

Components of Drippings:

- Fat: Used to create the roux, which thickens the gravy.

- Juices: Packed with flavor, these form the liquid base of the sauce.

- Fond: The browned bits stuck to the pan add depth and richness.

Pro Tip: Always scrape the fond from the pan to ensure the full flavor is incorporated into the gravy.

2. Basic Steps to Make Gravy

Making gravy from drippings involves three simple steps:

1. Collect the Drippings: After roasting, pour the drippings into a fat separator or bowl. Skim off excess fat, leaving behind the juices.

2. Deglaze the Pan: Place the roasting pan over medium heat and add a liquid (broth, wine, or water) to dissolve the fond. Scrape with a wooden spoon.

3. Thicken the Gravy: Create a roux with fat and flour or use a cornstarch slurry to achieve the desired consistency. Combine with the deglazed liquid and simmer.

Pro Tip: Adjust seasoning only after simmering, as reducing the liquid concentrates the flavors.

Recipes: Classic Gravy and Pan Sauces

1. Beef Au Jus

Beef au jus is a light, flavorful sauce served alongside roasted beef, especially prime rib. It enhances the meat's natural flavor without overwhelming it.

Ingredients:
- Pan drippings from roasted beef
- 2 cups beef stock or broth
- 1/4 cup red wine (optional)
- 1 teaspoon Worcestershire sauce
- Salt and black pepper to taste

Instructions:

1. Deglaze the Pan: Place the roasting pan over medium heat. Add red wine (if using) and scrape up the fond. Simmer until the liquid reduces by half.

2. Add Broth: Stir in the beef stock and Worcestershire sauce. Simmer for 5-10 minutes to combine flavors.

3. Strain: Pour the sauce through a fine-mesh sieve to remove solids.

4. Season: Add salt and black pepper to taste. Serve warm alongside roasted beef.

Pro Tip: For a richer au jus, whisk in a small pat of cold butter just before serving.

2. Turkey Gravy

Turkey gravy is a Thanksgiving staple, but it's equally at home on weeknight roasted chicken. This recipe balances the rich turkey flavor with a velvety smooth texture.

Ingredients:
- Pan drippings from roasted turkey

- 1/4 cup unsalted butter (or fat from the drippings)
- 1/4 cup all-purpose flour
- 2 cups turkey or chicken stock
- Salt, black pepper, and a pinch of thyme

Instructions:

1. Separate Drippings: Pour the drippings into a fat separator. Reserve the fat and liquid.

2. Make a Roux: In a saucepan, melt butter or the reserved fat over medium heat. Stir in flour and cook for 2-3 minutes until golden brown.

3. Add Stock: Slowly whisk in turkey stock and reserved juices, ensuring no lumps form.

4. Simmer and Season: Cook for 5-7 minutes until thickened. Season with salt, pepper, and thyme.

Pro Tip: For a more intense flavor, simmer the turkey stock with onion, garlic, and herbs before adding it to the roux.

3. Red Wine Reduction

This elegant pan sauce pairs beautifully with steak, lamb, or duck, delivering a deep, robust flavor.

Ingredients:
- 1/2 cup red wine
- 1 cup beef or chicken stock
- 1 shallot, finely chopped
- 1 tablespoon butter
- 1 teaspoon sugar (optional)
- Salt and black pepper to taste

Instructions:

1. Cook Shallots: In a skillet, melt butter over medium heat. Add shallots and sauté until softened.

2. Deglaze with Wine: Pour in red wine, scraping up the fond. Simmer until reduced by half.

3. Add Stock: Stir in the stock and continue to simmer until the sauce thickens slightly (5-7 minutes).

4. Season and Serve: Add sugar if needed to balance acidity. Season with salt and pepper. Serve warm.

Pro Tip: Swirl in a pat of cold butter before serving to give the sauce a glossy finish.

Tips for Achieving Smooth, Lump-Free Gravy

1. Use a Whisk

Whisking ensures the flour or cornstarch is evenly incorporated into the liquid, preventing lumps.

2. Add Liquid Gradually

Pour the liquid into the roux or slurry slowly, whisking constantly to create a smooth mixture.

3. Strain the Gravy

For an ultra-smooth texture, strain the gravy through a fine-mesh sieve to remove any lumps or solids.

4. Avoid Over-Thickening

Gravy continues to thicken as it cools, so stop cooking when it's slightly thinner than desired.

5. Fixing Lumpy Gravy

If lumps form, don't panic:

- Use an immersion blender to smooth the gravy.

- Push it through a sieve for a lump-free result.

Pro Tip: Always sift flour before using it to avoid clumps in the roux.

Pairing Gravy and Pan Sauces with Dishes

1. Proteins

- Beef Au Jus: Perfect for prime rib, roast beef, or French dip sandwiches.

- Turkey Gravy: Ideal for turkey, chicken, or even pork chops.

- Red Wine Reduction: Complements steak, lamb, or duck.

2. Side Dishes

- Mashed Potatoes: A natural pairing for turkey gravy or beef au jus.

- Roasted Vegetables: Drizzle red wine reduction over carrots or Brussels sprouts.

- Stuffing or Dressing: Turkey gravy ties these Thanksgiving staples together.

3. Bread

- Serve gravy with biscuits or rolls for dipping.

- Use red wine reduction as a spread for crusty bread in upscale appetizers.

Pro Tip: Use leftover gravy or pan sauce to enrich soups, stews, or casseroles.

Customizing Gravy and Pan Sauces

1. Add Herbs

Incorporate rosemary, thyme, or sage for an earthy flavor.

2. Experiment with Acidity

Use vinegar, citrus juice, or wine to balance the richness of the sauce.

3. Infuse Aromatics

Add garlic, shallots, or leeks to deepen the flavor profile.

Closing Thoughts

Classic gravies and pan sauces are the unsung heroes of the dinner table, turning simple meals into extraordinary experiences. By mastering the techniques outlined in this chapter and experimenting with the recipes, you can create sauces that elevate everything from holiday feasts to everyday dinners. Whether it's the comforting richness of turkey gravy, the elegance of a red wine reduction, or the simplicity of beef au jus, these sauces are sure to impress and satisfy. Let's keep exploring the world of sauces to uncover even more culinary possibilities!

Chapter 9: Luscious Dessert Sauces

Dessert sauces are the finishing touch that can elevate a simple treat into a decadent showstopper. Whether it's the velvety richness of chocolate ganache, the buttery sweetness of caramel, or the vibrant tang of a berry coulis, dessert sauces add layers of flavor, texture, and visual appeal. Perfectly crafted sauces are not only delicious but also versatile, serving as a complement to cakes, ice creams, pastries, and more.

In this chapter, we'll explore the art of making luscious dessert sauces, provide recipes for three timeless classics, and share techniques for achieving perfect textures every time. From mastering the glossy sheen of ganache to creating the smooth silkiness of caramel, you'll gain the skills to transform any dessert into a masterpiece.

Why Dessert Sauces Matter

1. Enhancing Flavor

Dessert sauces provide a burst of complementary or contrasting flavors, enhancing the overall taste of a dish.

- Chocolate Ganache: Adds richness and depth to cakes and pastries.
- Caramel Sauce: Balances sweetness with a hint of bitterness.
- Berry Coulis: Brightens desserts with tangy, fruity notes.

Pro Tip: Pair sauces with desserts that balance their flavors, like a tangy coulis with a rich cheesecake or caramel sauce with salty pecans.

2. Adding Texture

Beyond flavor, sauces bring a luxurious texture to desserts. Whether drizzled, swirled, or poured, their smooth consistency creates a delightful contrast with crunchy, soft, or flaky elements.

3. Creating Visual Appeal

A beautifully applied sauce adds an element of artistry to desserts. Swirls, drizzles, or pools of sauce can turn a simple plate into a visual feast.

Pro Tip: Use a squeeze bottle or a spoon to create intricate designs on the plate.

Essential Techniques for Perfect Dessert Sauces

1. Balancing Ingredients

Achieving the right balance of fat, sugar, and liquid is crucial for a dessert sauce's flavor and texture.

- Fat: Provides richness (e.g., cream, butter, chocolate).
- Sugar: Adds sweetness and can caramelize for depth.
- Liquid: Adjusts the consistency (e.g., milk, water, fruit juice).

Pro Tip: Start with less liquid and add gradually to avoid overly thin sauces.

2. Controlling Temperature

Temperature plays a critical role in achieving smooth, glossy textures:

- Low and Slow Heat: Prevents burning or curdling.
- Even Heating: Use a heavy-bottomed saucepan for consistent heat distribution.
- Cooling: Let sauces cool slightly before serving to thicken naturally.

3. Avoiding Common Mistakes

- Lumpy Sauces: Whisk continuously and strain if needed.
- Burnt Caramel: Keep an eye on the sugar, as it can burn quickly.
- Split Ganache: Use gentle heat and stir continuously to prevent separation.

Recipes: Classic Luscious Dessert Sauces

1. Chocolate Ganache

Chocolate ganache is a luxurious sauce that doubles as a glaze, filling, or frosting. Its velvety texture and deep chocolate flavor make it a dessert staple.

Ingredients:

- 8 ounces bittersweet or semisweet chocolate, chopped

- 1 cup heavy cream

- 1 tablespoon unsalted butter (optional, for extra sheen)

Instructions:

1. Heat Cream: In a small saucepan, heat cream over medium heat until it just begins to simmer (do not boil).

2. Melt Chocolate: Place chopped chocolate in a heatproof bowl. Pour hot cream over the chocolate and let sit for 2 minutes.

3. Stir Until Smooth: Gently whisk the mixture until smooth and glossy. Stir in butter if desired.

4. Cool: Allow to cool slightly before using as a sauce or glaze.

Pro Tip: For a thicker consistency, use a 2:1 chocolate-to-cream ratio.

2. Caramel Sauce

Caramel sauce strikes the perfect balance between buttery sweetness and a hint of bitterness, making it ideal for ice cream, pies, or pancakes.

Ingredients:

- 1 cup granulated sugar

- 1/4 cup water

- 1/2 cup heavy cream, warmed

- 2 tablespoons unsalted butter

- 1 teaspoon vanilla extract (optional)

- Pinch of salt

Instructions:

1. Cook Sugar: In a heavy-bottomed saucepan, combine sugar and water. Heat over medium heat, swirling (not stirring) until the sugar dissolves.

2. Caramelize: Increase heat to medium-high and cook until the sugar turns a deep amber color.

3. Add Cream: Remove from heat and carefully whisk in the warm cream (it will bubble vigorously).

4. Finish: Stir in butter, vanilla, and salt. Let cool before serving.

Pro Tip: Use salt sparingly to enhance the caramel's flavor without making it overly salty.

3. Berry Coulis

Berry coulis is a vibrant, fruit-forward sauce that adds a tangy contrast to rich desserts like cheesecake or panna cotta.

Ingredients:

- 2 cups fresh or frozen berries (strawberries, raspberries, or blueberries)
- 1/4 cup sugar (adjust based on berry sweetness)
- 1 tablespoon lemon juice
- 1 tablespoon water (optional, for thinning)

Instructions:

1. Cook Berries: In a saucepan, combine berries, sugar, and lemon juice. Cook over medium heat until the berries break down and release their juices (5-7 minutes).

2. Blend: Use an immersion blender or transfer the mixture to a blender to puree until smooth.

3. Strain: Press the mixture through a fine-mesh sieve to remove seeds.

4. Adjust Consistency: Stir in water if needed to reach your desired thickness.

Pro Tip: Add a splash of liqueur, such as Grand Marnier or Chambord, for a sophisticated twist.

Pairing Dessert Sauces with Dishes

1. Chocolate Ganache

- Cakes: Drizzle over chocolate or pound cakes.
    - Ice Cream: Use as a warm topping for vanilla or coffee ice cream.
    - Fruit: Dip strawberries, bananas, or cherries for a simple fondue.

2. Caramel Sauce

- Pies: Drizzle over apple or pecan pie for added decadence.
    - Pancakes: Use as a breakfast topping alongside whipped cream.
    - Cheesecake: Add a layer of caramel for a salty-sweet contrast.

3. Berry Coulis

- Cheesecake: Spoon over classic New York-style cheesecake.
    - Yogurt: Stir into Greek yogurt for a healthy dessert option.
    - Panna Cotta: Add a vibrant layer of coulis to creamy panna cotta.

Customizing Dessert Sauces

1. Adding Flavor Infusions

- Chocolate Ganache: Add espresso powder or orange zest for a twist.
    - Caramel Sauce: Infuse with cinnamon or vanilla bean.
    - Berry Coulis: Incorporate fresh herbs like mint or basil.

2. Experimenting with Sweetness

Adjust sugar levels to balance the sauce with your dessert.
    - Reduce sugar for tangy sauces.
    - Add honey or maple syrup for depth.

3. Exploring Textures

- For chunkier coulis, skip blending and strain only lightly.
    - Add chopped nuts or sea salt to caramel for crunch.

Storage and Reheating Tips

- Refrigeration: Store sauces in airtight containers in the fridge for up to one week.
    - Freezing: Freeze ganache or coulis in small portions for up to three months.
    - Reheating: Warm caramel and ganache gently over a double boiler or in the microwave, stirring frequently.

Closing Thoughts

Luscious dessert sauces are the perfect way to transform simple desserts into extraordinary creations. By mastering chocolate ganache, caramel sauce, and berry coulis, you'll have the tools to impress at any occasion. With their versatility, these sauces open the door to endless culinary creativity, allowing you to experiment with flavors, textures, and pairings. Let's keep exploring the world of sauces to uncover even more delicious possibilities!

Chapter 10: Boozy Sauces

Boozy sauces are a delightful way to elevate both sweet and savory dishes. By incorporating alcohol into sauces, you can introduce layers of complexity, enhance existing flavors, and create a luxurious finish for any meal. Whether you're drizzling bourbon caramel over a rich chocolate dessert, glazing a roast with a red wine reduction, or savoring the silky depth of a rum butter sauce, boozy sauces bring a distinctive edge to your culinary repertoire.

In this chapter, we'll explore the art of incorporating alcohol into sauces, provide step-by-step recipes for three versatile and indulgent boozy sauces, and share essential tips for balancing flavors while avoiding overpowering alcohol notes.

The Role of Alcohol in Sauces

1. Flavor Enhancement

Alcohol doesn't just add its own flavor—it enhances the other ingredients in a sauce. The volatile compounds in alcohol carry aroma and flavor molecules, amplifying the depth and richness of your dish.

Common Uses in Sweet Sauces:

- Bourbon or rum adds warmth and complexity.

- Liqueurs like Grand Marnier or Amaretto provide sweetness and a citrus or nutty profile.

Common Uses in Savory Sauces:

- Wine adds acidity and depth, balancing rich dishes.

- Spirits like brandy or whiskey create bold, robust notes.

2. Evaporation and Concentration

When alcohol is cooked, much of it evaporates, leaving behind a concentrated flavor.

- Light Cooking (Simmering): Retains more alcohol and a stronger flavor.

- Long Cooking (Reduction): Significantly reduces the alcohol content, leaving only the essence.

Pro Tip: For sauces with a subtle hint of alcohol, let the sauce simmer until most of the alcohol has burned off.

3. Pairing Alcohol with Ingredients

Choosing the right alcohol depends on the flavor profile of your sauce and dish:
- Bourbon: Pairs well with caramel, chocolate, or smoked meats.
- Rum: Complements tropical fruits, vanilla, or spiced desserts.
- Wine: Works for reductions and glazes, enhancing red meat or poultry.

Pro Tip: Always use alcohol that you enjoy drinking—its flavor will be prominent in the sauce.

Recipes: Classic Boozy Sauces

1. Bourbon Caramel Sauce

Bourbon caramel sauce is a luxurious addition to desserts like ice cream, bread pudding, or apple pie. Its deep, smoky flavor balances the buttery sweetness of caramel.

Ingredients:
- 1 cup granulated sugar
- 1/4 cup water
- 1/2 cup heavy cream, warmed
- 2 tablespoons unsalted butter
- 2 tablespoons bourbon
- Pinch of salt

Instructions:

1. Cook Sugar: Combine sugar and water in a heavy-bottomed saucepan. Heat over medium heat, swirling the pan occasionally, until the sugar dissolves.

2. Caramelize: Increase heat to medium-high and cook until the sugar turns a deep amber color.

3. Add Cream: Remove from heat and carefully whisk in the warm cream. The mixture will bubble vigorously.

4. Finish: Stir in butter, bourbon, and salt until smooth.

5. Cool: Let cool slightly before using. Store in the refrigerator for up to one week.

Pro Tip: For a smoky twist, use smoked bourbon or add a pinch of smoked paprika.

2. Rum Butter Sauce

Rum butter sauce is a decadent topping for bread pudding, pound cake, or grilled pineapple. The rum's warmth pairs beautifully with the buttery, velvety texture.

Ingredients:
- 1/2 cup unsalted butter
- 1 cup brown sugar
- 1/2 cup heavy cream
- 2 tablespoons dark rum
- 1 teaspoon vanilla extract
- Pinch of cinnamon (optional)

Instructions:

1. Melt Butter: In a saucepan, melt butter over medium heat.

2. Dissolve Sugar: Stir in brown sugar and cook until fully dissolved.

3. Add Cream: Slowly pour in heavy cream, whisking continuously to combine.

4. Incorporate Rum and Vanilla: Stir in rum, vanilla extract, and cinnamon if using.

5. Simmer: Cook for 2-3 minutes, then remove from heat.

Pro Tip: Use spiced rum for added depth and complexity.

3. Red Wine Glaze

This glossy, rich glaze is ideal for roasted meats, vegetables, or as a finishing touch for risottos and pasta.

Ingredients:
- 1 cup red wine (e.g., Cabernet Sauvignon or Merlot)

- 1/2 cup beef or chicken stock
- 1 small shallot, finely chopped
- 1 tablespoon butter
- 1 teaspoon sugar (optional)
- Salt and black pepper to taste

Instructions:

1. Sauté Shallots: Melt butter in a saucepan over medium heat. Add shallots and sauté until softened.

2. Deglaze with Wine: Pour in red wine, scraping up any browned bits from the pan. Simmer until reduced by half.

3. Add Stock: Stir in stock and continue simmering until the sauce thickens slightly.

4. Season: Add sugar (if needed), salt, and black pepper to taste.

Pro Tip: For extra richness, whisk in a pat of cold butter just before serving.

Balancing Flavors in Boozy Sauces

1. Sweet vs. Savory

When incorporating alcohol into sauces, balance is key:
- Sweet Sauces: Add a pinch of salt to counteract sweetness.
- Savory Sauces: Use a touch of sugar or honey to balance acidity.

2. Adjusting Intensity

- Too Strong: Cook longer to reduce the alcohol content and mellow the flavor.
- Too Weak: Add a splash of alcohol at the end of cooking for a more pronounced flavor.

Pro Tip: Always taste as you go to achieve the desired balance.

3. Enhancing with Aromatics

Aromatics like vanilla, cinnamon, garlic, or shallots can complement the alcohol's flavor profile.
- Bourbon: Pair with vanilla or nutmeg.
- Rum: Combine with cinnamon or cloves.

- Wine: Use garlic or rosemary for savory sauces.

Tips for Working with Alcohol in Sauces

1. Use High-Quality Alcohol

Cheap alcohol can add harsh flavors to your sauce. Opt for mid-range or higher-quality spirits and wines.

2. Cook Off the Alcohol (When Necessary)

For subtle flavor, simmer the sauce to burn off most of the alcohol content.

3. Consider Pairings

Match the sauce to the dish's flavor profile:

- Sweet dishes pair well with bourbon or rum-based sauces.
- Savory dishes shine with wine or brandy reductions.

Pairing Boozy Sauces with Dishes

1. Bourbon Caramel Sauce

- Ice Cream: Drizzle over vanilla or butter pecan ice cream.
- Pies: Add to apple pie or pecan pie for extra depth.
- Cakes: Pair with chocolate or banana cakes.

2. Rum Butter Sauce

- Bread Pudding: A classic pairing that enhances its richness.
- Tropical Fruits: Drizzle over grilled pineapple or bananas foster.
- Pancakes: Use as a decadent breakfast topping.

3. Red Wine Glaze

- Steak: A natural pairing with grilled or seared beef.
- Lamb: Complements the gamey flavor of roasted lamb.
- Vegetables: Drizzle over roasted root vegetables or mushrooms.

Customizing Boozy Sauces

1. Experimenting with Alcohols

- Substitute whiskey for bourbon or brandy for rum to create new flavor profiles.

2. Adjusting Sweetness

- Add more sugar for desserts or a touch of honey for savory glazes.

3. Adding Spices and Herbs

- Cinnamon, cloves, nutmeg, or fresh rosemary can deepen the flavor of boozy sauces.

Storage and Reheating Tips

- Refrigeration: Store sauces in airtight containers for up to one week.

- Freezing: Freeze in small portions for up to three months.

- Reheating: Warm gently over low heat, adding a splash of liquid to restore consistency if needed.

Closing Thoughts

Boozy sauces bring sophistication and bold flavors to both sweet and savory dishes. By mastering recipes like bourbon caramel, rum butter sauce, and red wine glaze, you can enhance your culinary repertoire and impress your guests. With a balance of flavors, thoughtful pairings, and creative customization, these sauces are sure to transform your meals into unforgettable experiences. Let's continue exploring the art of sauce-making to uncover even more ways to elevate your cooking!

Chapter 11: Fruit-Based Sauces

Fruit-based sauces are a celebration of nature's sweetness, vibrancy, and versatility. By harnessing the natural flavors of fruits, these sauces can elevate savory dishes, complement desserts, and enhance the richness of cheeses. From the tropical allure of mango chutney to the tangy zest of cranberry sauce and the comforting warmth of apple compote, fruit-based sauces are a must-have in any culinary repertoire.

This chapter explores the art of creating vibrant fruit-based sauces, provides detailed recipes for three timeless classics, and offers pairing suggestions to help you unlock their full potential.

Why Fruit-Based Sauces Matter

1. A Symphony of Natural Sweetness

Fruits bring a natural sweetness that is both nuanced and refreshing. Unlike processed sugars, fruits provide depth and complexity, often balancing sweetness with acidity or bitterness.

Examples:

- Cranberries: Naturally tart with a hint of bitterness, perfect for balancing rich proteins like turkey or pork.

- Mangoes: Sweet and tropical, adding brightness to spicy dishes.

- Apples: Mild and versatile, ideal for warm, comforting sauces.

Pro Tip: Use ripe, fresh fruits whenever possible to maximize flavor and sweetness.

2. Versatility Across Dishes

Fruit-based sauces shine in a wide variety of culinary applications:

- Savory: Pair with roasted meats or seafood for a hint of sweetness.

- Desserts: Drizzle over ice cream, cakes, or pancakes for a fruity twist.

- Cheese Boards: Complement the creaminess of cheeses with tangy or spiced fruit sauces.

Pro Tip: Adjust sugar and spice levels to tailor the sauce to your dish.

3. Nutritional Benefits

Beyond their flavor, fruits add a healthy touch to sauces, contributing vitamins, minerals, and antioxidants. They're a flavorful way to reduce the reliance on processed sugars in your cooking.

Essential Techniques for Fruit-Based Sauces

1. Balancing Sweetness and Acidity

Fruits naturally contain sugars and acids, but balancing them is crucial for creating a well-rounded sauce.

- Sweetness Adjustments: Add honey, sugar, or maple syrup to tame overly tart fruits.

- Acidity Adjustments: Incorporate lemon juice, vinegar, or wine to brighten overly sweet sauces.

Pro Tip: Always taste as you go and adjust the balance incrementally.

2. Controlling Texture

The texture of a fruit-based sauce can vary from smooth and silky to chunky and rustic:

- Smooth Sauces: Blend and strain for a refined finish, ideal for desserts.

- Chunky Sauces: Leave whole fruit pieces for a rustic feel, perfect for savory pairings.

Pro Tip: Thicken sauces with cornstarch, pectin, or reduction for desired consistency.

3. Layering Flavors with Spices and Herbs

Adding spices or herbs enhances the complexity of fruit sauces:

- Warm Spices: Cinnamon, cloves, and nutmeg work well with apples and cranberries.

- Fresh Herbs: Mint, cilantro, or thyme complement tropical fruits like mango.

Pro Tip: Infuse spices and herbs gently to avoid overpowering the fruit's natural flavor.

Recipes: Classic Fruit-Based Sauces

1. Mango Chutney

Mango chutney is a vibrant, sweet, and tangy sauce with a hint of spice, perfect for pairing with Indian curries, grilled chicken, or roasted vegetables.

Ingredients:

- 2 ripe mangoes, peeled and diced
- 1/4 cup sugar
- 1/4 cup white vinegar
- 1 small onion, finely chopped
- 1 garlic clove, minced
- 1 teaspoon grated ginger
- 1/2 teaspoon cumin powder
- 1/4 teaspoon chili flakes (optional)
- Pinch of salt

Instructions:

1. Cook Aromatics: In a saucepan, sauté onion, garlic, and ginger until softened.

2. Add Mango and Spices: Stir in mango, sugar, vinegar, cumin, chili flakes, and salt.

3. Simmer: Cook over medium heat, stirring occasionally, until the mixture thickens (15-20 minutes).

4. Cool and Store: Let cool before transferring to a jar. Store in the refrigerator for up to two weeks.

Pro Tip: Add raisins or chopped nuts for extra texture and flavor.

2. Cranberry Sauce

Cranberry sauce is a Thanksgiving classic, but its tart, tangy flavor pairs beautifully with pork, poultry, and creamy cheeses year-round.

Ingredients:
- 12 ounces fresh or frozen cranberries
- 1/2 cup orange juice
- 1/2 cup water
- 3/4 cup sugar (adjust to taste)
- 1 teaspoon orange zest
- Pinch of cinnamon (optional)

Instructions:

1. Combine Ingredients: In a saucepan, combine cranberries, orange juice, water, sugar, orange zest, and cinnamon.

2. Cook: Bring to a boil, then reduce heat and simmer until the cranberries burst and the sauce thickens (10-15 minutes).

3. Cool: Let cool before serving. Refrigerate leftovers for up to one week.

Pro Tip: Blend the sauce for a smoother texture or leave it chunky for a more rustic feel.

3. Apple Compote

Apple compote is a warm, comforting sauce with a subtle sweetness, ideal for topping pancakes, waffles, or pork chops.

Ingredients:
- 4 medium apples, peeled, cored, and diced
- 1/4 cup brown sugar
- 1/4 cup water or apple juice
- 1/2 teaspoon cinnamon
- 1/4 teaspoon nutmeg
- 1 teaspoon lemon juice

Instructions:

1. Cook Apples: In a saucepan, combine apples, brown sugar, water, cinnamon, and nutmeg. Cook over medium heat until the apples soften (10-15 minutes).

2. Mash or Leave Chunky: Mash slightly with a fork for a chunky sauce or puree for smoothness.

3. Finish with Lemon: Stir in lemon juice and adjust sweetness if needed.

Pro Tip: Add a splash of Calvados (apple brandy) for an adult twist.

Pairing Fruit Sauces with Dishes

1. Proteins

- Mango Chutney: Pairs well with grilled chicken, pork chops, or salmon.
    - Cranberry Sauce: Complements roasted turkey, duck, or glazed ham.
    - Apple Compote: Works beautifully with pork loin, sausages, or roasted duck.

2. Desserts

- Mango Chutney: Adds a tangy contrast to vanilla ice cream or coconut panna cotta.
    - Cranberry Sauce: Perfect for cheesecakes, trifles, or pound cakes.
    - Apple Compote: A cozy topping for pancakes, waffles, or cinnamon-spiced oatmeal.

3. Cheeses

- Mango Chutney: Pairs with sharp cheddars or creamy Brie.
    - Cranberry Sauce: Enhances creamy goat cheese or tangy blue cheese.
    - Apple Compote: Complements aged Gouda or nutty Parmesan.
    Pro Tip: Serve fruit sauces on a cheese board alongside nuts, crackers, and fresh fruits.

Customizing Fruit-Based Sauces

1. Experimenting with Fruits

Swap or combine fruits to create new flavors:
    - Mango Chutney: Replace mango with peaches or apricots.
    - Cranberry Sauce: Mix in pomegranate seeds or raspberries.

- Apple Compote: Add pears for a sweeter twist.

2. Adjusting Sweetness

- Use honey, agave, or maple syrup for natural sweetness.
    - For tart fruits, increase sugar or blend with naturally sweet fruits like bananas.

3. Adding Texture

- Include nuts, seeds, or dried fruits for a crunchy contrast.
    - Keep fruit chunks intact for a rustic look.

Storage and Reheating Tips

- Refrigeration: Store sauces in airtight containers for up to one week.
    - Freezing: Freeze in small portions for up to three months.
    - Reheating: Warm gently over low heat, adding water or juice to adjust consistency.

Closing Thoughts

Fruit-based sauces bring color, flavor, and versatility to any dish. By mastering recipes like mango chutney, cranberry sauce, and apple compote, you'll have a repertoire of vibrant, natural sweeteners that can enhance savory dishes, desserts, and cheese boards alike. Experiment with seasonal fruits, spices, and textures to make these sauces your own. Let's continue exploring the endless possibilities of sauces to enrich your culinary journey!

Chapter 12: Classic Salad Dressings

Salad dressings are more than just condiments; they're the essence of a great salad, transforming simple greens into a burst of flavor. While store-bought dressings offer convenience, homemade versions far surpass them in taste, quality, and versatility. From the creamy richness of Caesar dressing to the tangy decadence of blue cheese and the universal appeal of ranch, classic salad dressings are essential in any culinary repertoire.

In this chapter, we'll explore the secrets of crafting homemade dressings, provide detailed recipes for three beloved classics, and teach you how to balance fat, acid, and seasonings to create the perfect dressing every time.

Why Make Homemade Salad Dressings?

1. Superior Flavor and Freshness

Homemade dressings offer a freshness and depth of flavor that store-bought versions simply can't match.

- Customizable: Adjust sweetness, acidity, or saltiness to your liking.

- No Preservatives: Free of artificial ingredients or stabilizers.

Pro Tip: Use high-quality oils, vinegars, and fresh ingredients for the best results.

2. Versatility Beyond Salads

Classic salad dressings are not limited to greens—they double as marinades, dips, or sandwich spreads. For example:

- Caesar Dressing: Works as a spread for wraps or a dip for roasted vegetables.

- Ranch: A classic dip for wings, fries, or fresh vegetables.

- Blue Cheese: Ideal for drizzling over burgers or steak.

3. Cost-Effective and Sustainable

Making dressings at home is often more economical and reduces single-use plastic waste from store-bought bottles.

The Basics of Salad Dressing: Balancing Fat, Acid, and Seasonings

1. The Building Blocks of a Dressing

A great salad dressing balances three key components:

1. Fat: Provides richness and body (e.g., olive oil, mayonnaise, or yogurt).

2. Acid: Adds tang and brightness (e.g., vinegar, lemon juice).

3. Seasonings: Enhances and complements the flavors (e.g., salt, pepper, garlic).

Pro Tip: A typical ratio for vinaigrettes is 3 parts fat to 1 part acid, but creamy dressings often use a 2:1 ratio of fat to acid.

2. Emulsification: The Science of Blending

Emulsification is the process of combining oil and water-based ingredients into a cohesive mixture.

- Temporary Emulsion: Achieved by whisking oil and vinegar; separates over time.

- Permanent Emulsion: Created with stabilizers like mustard or egg yolks, ensuring a smooth, creamy texture.

Pro Tip: Whisk or blend vigorously when incorporating oil to create a stable emulsion.

3. Adjusting Flavor Profiles

Taste as you go and tweak the dressing to suit your palate:

- Add honey or sugar for sweetness.

- Incorporate herbs or spices for complexity.

- Use anchovies, capers, or cheese for a savory punch.

Recipes: Classic Salad Dressings

1. Caesar Dressing

Rich, creamy, and packed with umami, Caesar dressing is a timeless favorite for salads, wraps, or dipping sauces.

Ingredients:

- 2 egg yolks (or 1 tablespoon mayonnaise for a safer option)
- 1 tablespoon Dijon mustard
- 1 garlic clove, minced
- 2 anchovy fillets, minced (or 1 teaspoon anchovy paste)
- 1/4 cup grated Parmesan cheese
- 2 tablespoons lemon juice
- 1/2 cup olive oil
- Salt and black pepper to taste

Instructions:

1. Create Base: In a bowl, whisk together egg yolks, Dijon mustard, garlic, and anchovies until smooth.

2. Add Lemon and Parmesan: Stir in lemon juice and Parmesan cheese.

3. Emulsify: Slowly drizzle in olive oil while whisking continuously until thick and creamy.

4. Season: Adjust with salt and pepper to taste.

Pro Tip: Use a blender for a smoother texture and faster emulsification.

2. Ranch Dressing

Cool, creamy, and herby, ranch dressing is a versatile staple, perfect for salads, dips, and spreads.

Ingredients:

- 1/2 cup mayonnaise
- 1/2 cup buttermilk (or regular milk for a thinner consistency)
- 1/4 cup sour cream
- 1 teaspoon garlic powder
- 1 teaspoon onion powder
- 1 teaspoon dried dill
- 1 teaspoon dried parsley

- Salt and black pepper to taste

Instructions:

1. Mix Base: In a bowl, whisk together mayonnaise, buttermilk, and sour cream until smooth.

2. Add Seasonings: Stir in garlic powder, onion powder, dill, and parsley.

3. Season: Adjust with salt and pepper to taste. Chill for 30 minutes before serving.

Pro Tip: Add fresh chopped herbs for a brighter flavor.

3. Blue Cheese Dressing

Bold and tangy, blue cheese dressing pairs beautifully with wedge salads, wings, or steak.

Ingredients:

- 1/2 cup mayonnaise
- 1/4 cup sour cream
- 1/4 cup buttermilk
- 1/2 cup crumbled blue cheese
- 1 teaspoon white vinegar
- Salt and black pepper to taste

Instructions:

1. Combine Base: In a bowl, whisk together mayonnaise, sour cream, and buttermilk.

2. Add Blue Cheese: Fold in blue cheese crumbles.

3. Adjust Tanginess: Stir in white vinegar and season with salt and pepper.

Pro Tip: Let the dressing sit for at least 30 minutes to allow the flavors to meld.

Pairing Salad Dressings with Greens and Dishes

1. Caesar Dressing

- Greens: Crisp romaine lettuce or kale.
  - Proteins: Grilled chicken, shrimp, or salmon.
  - Extras: Croutons, shaved Parmesan, or anchovies.

2. Ranch Dressing

- Greens: Iceberg, spinach, or mixed greens.
    - Proteins: Fried chicken, bacon, or hard-boiled eggs.
    - Extras: Chopped carrots, celery, or cherry tomatoes.

3. Blue Cheese Dressing

- Greens: Iceberg or butter lettuce.
    - Proteins: Steak, grilled chicken, or buffalo wings.
    - Extras: Crumbled bacon, red onions, or walnuts.

Tips for Perfect Homemade Dressings

1. Use Fresh Ingredients
    Fresh garlic, herbs, and high-quality oils make a noticeable difference in flavor.
    2. Achieve the Right Consistency
    Adjust the thickness of your dressing by adding more liquid (e.g., milk or vinegar) or thickening agents (e.g., mayonnaise or yogurt).
    3. Make in Advance
    Allow dressings to sit for at least 30 minutes before serving to let the flavors meld.
    4. Store Properly
    Refrigerate dressings in airtight containers for up to one week. Stir or shake before using.

Customizing Classic Dressings

1. Experiment with Add-Ins
    - Add anchovy paste or capers to Caesar dressing for extra umami.
    - Mix fresh herbs like chives or cilantro into ranch dressing.
    - Stir honey or hot sauce into blue cheese dressing for a unique twist.
    2. Adjust Acidity
    - Use lime juice or rice vinegar for a milder tang.
    - Add a pinch of sugar to balance overly acidic dressings.

3. Swap Fats

- Substitute Greek yogurt for mayonnaise or sour cream for a lighter option.

- Use avocado oil or walnut oil for a distinctive flavor.

Closing Thoughts

Classic salad dressings are an essential component of any cook's repertoire, bringing vibrancy and flavor to a wide range of dishes. By mastering Caesar, ranch, and blue cheese dressings, you'll gain the skills to elevate salads, dips, and marinades with ease. With endless opportunities for customization and versatility, these dressings can transform even the simplest meals into something extraordinary. Let's continue exploring the world of sauces and dressings to uncover even more culinary possibilities!

Chapter 13: Light and Healthy Vinaigrettes

Vinaigrettes are the epitome of light and versatile salad dressings, combining the richness of oil with the tanginess of vinegar to enhance the flavors of greens, vegetables, and grains. Unlike creamy dressings, vinaigrettes are naturally lighter and can be customized endlessly with herbs, spices, and sweeteners. From the zesty brightness of lemon vinaigrette to the depth of balsamic and the nutty complexity of Asian sesame dressing, these classic recipes form the backbone of any salad lover's repertoire.

In this chapter, we'll explore the art of perfecting oil-and-vinegar ratios, provide recipes for three iconic vinaigrettes, and teach you how to experiment with herbs, spices, and sweeteners to create your own signature dressings.

What Makes Vinaigrettes Special?

1. Simplicity and Versatility

Vinaigrettes are quick and easy to make, requiring just a few basic ingredients. They can elevate everything from a humble green salad to roasted vegetables and grains.

Key Features:

- Light Texture: Their low-fat, high-acid nature makes them a healthier option.

- Customizable Flavor: Endless possibilities with different oils, vinegars, and seasonings.

- Multifunctional: Use as a dressing, marinade, or finishing drizzle.

2. Health Benefits

Vinaigrettes are a great way to incorporate healthy fats, antioxidants, and nutrients into your diet.

- Healthy Oils: Olive oil, avocado oil, and sesame oil are rich in monounsaturated fats.

- Vinegar Benefits: Apple cider and balsamic vinegar may support digestion and blood sugar regulation.

Pro Tip: To keep it light, use less oil and add water or broth to thin the vinaigrette.

Perfecting Oil-and-Vinegar Ratios

1. The Classic Ratio

The standard oil-to-vinegar ratio is *3 parts oil to 1 part vinegar*, but this is just a guideline. Adjust to suit your taste and the ingredients in your salad.

- For Milder Flavors: Stick to the classic ratio.

- For Tangier Vinaigrettes: Use equal parts oil and vinegar or increase the vinegar slightly.

Pro Tip: Taste your vinaigrette on a leaf of salad to ensure the flavor complements the dish.

2. Emulsifying Vinaigrettes

Vinaigrettes naturally separate into oil and vinegar layers. Emulsifiers help them blend smoothly:

- Common Emulsifiers: Mustard, honey, and egg yolk.

- Technique: Whisk or shake vigorously to create a temporary emulsion.

Pro Tip: A blender or immersion blender creates a more stable, creamy vinaigrette.

Recipes: Light and Healthy Vinaigrettes

1. Lemon Vinaigrette

This zesty dressing brightens up greens, grains, and grilled vegetables with its fresh citrus flavor.

Ingredients:

- 1/4 cup olive oil

- 2 tablespoons fresh lemon juice

- 1 teaspoon Dijon mustard

- 1 teaspoon honey (optional)

- Salt and black pepper to taste

Instructions:

1. Combine Ingredients: In a small bowl, whisk together lemon juice, Dijon mustard, honey, salt, and pepper.

2. Add Oil Gradually: Slowly drizzle in olive oil while whisking continuously until emulsified.

3. Taste and Adjust: Add more lemon juice or honey to balance acidity and sweetness.

Pro Tip: Add minced garlic or fresh herbs like dill or parsley for extra flavor.

2. Balsamic Vinaigrette

Rich and tangy, balsamic vinaigrette pairs beautifully with hearty salads, roasted vegetables, and caprese dishes.

Ingredients:

- 1/4 cup balsamic vinegar

- 3/4 cup olive oil

- 1 teaspoon Dijon mustard

- 1 teaspoon honey or maple syrup

- Salt and black pepper to taste

Instructions:

1. Mix Base Ingredients: In a bowl, whisk together balsamic vinegar, Dijon mustard, honey, salt, and pepper.

2. Incorporate Oil: Gradually whisk in olive oil until smooth and emulsified.

3. Taste and Adjust: Balance sweetness and tang with additional honey or vinegar if needed.

Pro Tip: Add a pinch of crushed red pepper flakes for a subtle kick.

3. Asian Sesame Dressing

This nutty, tangy vinaigrette is perfect for Asian-inspired salads, slaws, or noodle dishes.

Ingredients:

- 2 tablespoons sesame oil

- 2 tablespoons rice vinegar

- 1 tablespoon soy sauce
- 1 tablespoon honey or brown sugar
- 1 teaspoon grated fresh ginger
- 1 teaspoon minced garlic
- Optional: 1 tablespoon toasted sesame seeds

Instructions:

1. Mix Base Ingredients: In a bowl, combine sesame oil, rice vinegar, soy sauce, honey, ginger, and garlic.

2. Blend or Whisk: Whisk until smooth, or blend for a creamier texture.

3. Add Sesame Seeds: Stir in toasted sesame seeds if desired.

Pro Tip: Adjust sweetness and saltiness to taste, depending on the type of soy sauce used.

Adding Variety with Herbs, Spices, and Sweeteners

1. Fresh and Dried Herbs

Herbs bring vibrancy and complexity to vinaigrettes:

- Fresh: Parsley, cilantro, dill, basil, or mint.
- Dried: Oregano, thyme, rosemary, or herbes de Provence.

Pro Tip: Use fresh herbs for delicate salads and dried herbs for robust flavors.

2. Spices and Aromatics

Spices and aromatics add depth and warmth:

- Spices: Paprika, cumin, or coriander.
- Aromatics: Minced garlic, shallots, or ginger.

Pro Tip: Lightly toast spices before adding them to release their full flavor.

3. Sweeteners

Sweeteners balance acidity and round out flavors:

- Liquid Sweeteners: Honey, agave, or maple syrup.
- Granulated Sweeteners: Brown sugar or coconut sugar (dissolve thoroughly).

Pro Tip: Pair sweeteners with complementary acids, such as honey with lemon or maple syrup with balsamic vinegar.

Pairing Vinaigrettes with Salads and Dishes

1. Lemon Vinaigrette

- Salads: Arugula, spinach, or kale.
    - Grains: Quinoa or farro.
    - Proteins: Grilled shrimp, chicken, or salmon.

2. Balsamic Vinaigrette

- Salads: Mixed greens with goat cheese, walnuts, and cranberries.
    - Vegetables: Roasted Brussels sprouts or asparagus.
    - Caprese: Drizzle over tomatoes, mozzarella, and basil.

3. Asian Sesame Dressing

- Salads: Cabbage slaw or mixed greens with mandarin oranges.
    - Noodles: Toss with soba or rice noodles.
    - Proteins: Grilled tofu, chicken, or shrimp.

Tips for Perfect Vinaigrettes

1. Taste as You Go

Adjust oil, vinegar, and seasonings incrementally to achieve the perfect balance.

2. Experiment with Oils and Vinegars

- Oils: Try avocado oil, walnut oil, or grapeseed oil for unique flavors.
- Vinegars: Use apple cider, sherry, or champagne vinegar for variety.

3. Make in Advance

Let vinaigrettes sit for 30 minutes before serving to allow the flavors to meld.

4. Store Properly

Refrigerate vinaigrettes in an airtight container for up to one week. Shake well before use.

Customizing Vinaigrettes

1. Add Citrus Zest
    Incorporate lemon, lime, or orange zest for a burst of freshness.
    2. Spice It Up
    Add chili flakes, sriracha, or a splash of hot sauce for heat.
    3. Boost Creaminess
    Blend in avocado, Greek yogurt, or tahini for a richer texture.

Closing Thoughts

Light and healthy vinaigrettes are essential for adding brightness and flavor to salads, grains, and more. By mastering recipes like lemon vinaigrette, balsamic vinaigrette, and Asian sesame dressing, and experimenting with herbs, spices, and sweeteners, you'll create dressings that elevate any dish. With their simplicity, versatility, and health benefits, vinaigrettes are a cornerstone of modern cooking. Let's continue exploring the world of sauces and dressings to uncover even more delicious possibilities!

Chapter 14: Flavorful Marinades

Marinades are a powerful culinary tool that can transform simple ingredients into flavorful and tender dishes. By combining acids, fats, herbs, and spices, marinades penetrate meats, seafood, and vegetables, enhancing their taste and texture. Whether you're grilling, roasting, or stir-frying, a well-crafted marinade lays the foundation for an unforgettable meal.

In this chapter, we'll explore how marinades work, provide detailed recipes for teriyaki, Greek yogurt, and citrus herb marinades, and share tips on marinating times and avoiding overpowering flavors.

The Science of Marinades

1. How Marinades Work

Marinades enhance food in two key ways:

- Flavor Infusion: Acids and spices seep into the surface of the food, adding layers of taste.

- Tenderization: Acids break down proteins in meat, resulting in a softer texture.

Key Components of a Marinade:

1. Acid: Vinegar, citrus juice, yogurt, or wine to tenderize and brighten flavors.

2. Fat: Oil or yogurt to carry flavors and prevent drying out.

3. Seasonings: Herbs, spices, garlic, and onion for depth and complexity.

4. Sweeteners (Optional): Honey, brown sugar, or molasses to balance acidity and enhance browning.

Pro Tip: Avoid overly acidic marinades for delicate proteins like fish, as they can cause the texture to become mushy.

2. Factors That Influence Marinating

Several factors affect how well marinades work:

- Type of Protein: Dense meats like beef take longer to absorb flavors than chicken or fish.

- Cut of Meat: Smaller or thinner cuts marinate faster due to increased surface area.

- Time: Over-marinating can lead to overly soft textures, especially for proteins like fish or seafood.

Recipes: Classic and Versatile Marinades

1. Teriyaki Marinade

This sweet and savory marinade is a Japanese classic, ideal for chicken, beef, salmon, or tofu.

Ingredients:
- 1/4 cup soy sauce
- 1/4 cup mirin (or substitute with rice vinegar + 1 tablespoon sugar)
- 2 tablespoons brown sugar or honey
- 2 tablespoons sesame oil
- 2 garlic cloves, minced
- 1 teaspoon grated fresh ginger

Instructions:

1. Combine Ingredients: Whisk together soy sauce, mirin, sugar, sesame oil, garlic, and ginger in a bowl.

2. Marinate: Pour over your protein or vegetables, ensuring even coverage.

3. Marinating Time:
- Chicken: 2-4 hours
- Beef: 4-6 hours
- Fish/Seafood: 15-30 minutes
- Vegetables: 30 minutes

Pro Tip: Reserve a portion of the marinade before adding raw meat to use as a glaze or dipping sauce.

2. Greek Yogurt Marinade

The creamy tang of Greek yogurt pairs beautifully with Middle Eastern and Mediterranean flavors, making it perfect for chicken, lamb, or vegetables.

Ingredients:
- 1 cup plain Greek yogurt

- 2 tablespoons olive oil
- 2 tablespoons lemon juice
- 3 garlic cloves, minced
- 1 teaspoon dried oregano
- 1 teaspoon ground cumin
- 1/2 teaspoon smoked paprika
- Salt and black pepper to taste

Instructions:

1. Mix Base: In a bowl, whisk together yogurt, olive oil, lemon juice, garlic, and spices.

2. Marinate: Coat the protein or vegetables evenly with the mixture.

3. Marinating Time:

- Chicken: 4-6 hours or overnight
- Lamb: 6-8 hours or overnight
- Vegetables: 30 minutes

Pro Tip: The lactic acid in yogurt tenderizes proteins gently, making it ideal for tougher cuts of meat.

3. Citrus Herb Marinade

Bright and refreshing, this marinade is perfect for seafood, chicken, or roasted vegetables.

Ingredients:

- 1/4 cup olive oil
- 2 tablespoons lemon juice
- 2 tablespoons orange juice
- 1 tablespoon white wine vinegar
- 2 garlic cloves, minced
- 1 tablespoon chopped fresh parsley
- 1 teaspoon thyme leaves (fresh or dried)
- 1 teaspoon honey
- Salt and black pepper to taste

Instructions:

1. Combine Ingredients: Whisk together all ingredients in a small bowl.

2. Marinate: Pour over your protein or vegetables, ensuring full coverage.

3. Marinating Time:

- Chicken: 2-4 hours

- Fish/Seafood: 15-30 minutes

- Vegetables: 20-30 minutes

Pro Tip: Citrus marinades work best when used for short durations, as prolonged exposure can "cook" proteins like fish.

Tips for Proper Marinating

1. Use the Right Container

Always marinate in non-reactive containers like glass, ceramic, or food-safe plastic. Avoid metal containers, as acids can react with metal and alter the flavor.

2. Ensure Even Coverage

Flip or stir the food occasionally to ensure the marinade coats all sides evenly.

3. Refrigerate While Marinating

Keep marinated foods in the refrigerator to prevent bacterial growth.

4. Avoid Over-Marinating

Over-marinating can lead to overly soft or mushy textures, especially in seafood or thin cuts of meat.

Recommended Times:

- Chicken: 2-6 hours

- Beef: 4-24 hours (depending on cut)

- Fish/Seafood: 15-30 minutes

- Vegetables: 20-30 minutes

Avoiding Overpowering Flavors

1. Balance is Key

Overloading a marinade with strong flavors like garlic, soy sauce, or vinegar can overshadow the natural taste of the food.

Pro Tip: Use bold ingredients sparingly and balance them with neutral elements like oil or yogurt.

2. Reserve Some Marinade

Set aside a portion of the marinade before adding raw ingredients to use as a finishing sauce or glaze.

3. Taste Before Marinating

Mix and taste the marinade before adding it to your food. Adjust flavors if necessary by adding more acid, sweetness, or salt.

Pairing Marinades with Proteins and Vegetables

1. Teriyaki Marinade

- Proteins: Chicken thighs, beef stir-fry strips, salmon fillets, or tofu.
    - Vegetables: Bell peppers, zucchini, or broccoli for stir-frying or grilling.

2. Greek Yogurt Marinade

- Proteins: Chicken kebabs, lamb chops, or pork tenderloin.
    - Vegetables: Eggplant, mushrooms, or cauliflower for roasting.

3. Citrus Herb Marinade

- Proteins: White fish (cod, tilapia), shrimp, or chicken breasts.
    - Vegetables: Asparagus, cherry tomatoes, or green beans.

Creative Marinade Variations

1. Sweet and Spicy Marinade

- Ingredients: Honey, sriracha, lime juice, soy sauce.
    - Uses: Perfect for chicken wings or grilled shrimp.

2. Smoky Barbecue Marinade

- Ingredients: Smoked paprika, ketchup, brown sugar, apple cider vinegar.
    - Uses: Great for ribs, pork chops, or tofu.

3. Mediterranean Marinade

- Ingredients: Olive oil, lemon juice, garlic, rosemary, and oregano.
    - Uses: Ideal for lamb, chicken, or roasted vegetables.

Storage and Safety Tips

- Discard Used Marinade: Never reuse marinade that has come into contact with raw meat.
    - Make Extra for Sauce: Set aside a portion of fresh marinade for glazing or dipping.
    - Store Properly: Refrigerate unused marinade for up to one week or freeze for later use.

Closing Thoughts

Marinades are a simple yet transformative way to elevate the flavor and texture of your dishes. By mastering recipes like teriyaki, Greek yogurt, and citrus herb marinades, and following best practices for marinating times and safety, you can create meals that are bursting with flavor. Whether you're grilling, roasting, or stir-frying, a great marinade sets the stage for a truly memorable culinary experience. Let's continue exploring the art of enhancing food through the power of marinades!

Chapter 15: Customizing and Innovating Sauces

Sauces and dressings are the cornerstone of culinary creativity, transforming simple ingredients into extraordinary dishes. While mastering classic recipes is essential, the true art lies in customizing and innovating to create your own signature flavors. Whether you're balancing sweetness with acidity, perfecting spice levels, or drawing inspiration from global cuisines, the possibilities for crafting unique sauces are endless.

This chapter delves into advanced techniques for customizing sauces and dressings, offers tips on adjusting consistency and flavor profiles, and explores global influences to expand your sauce repertoire.

Why Customize and Innovate Sauces?

1. Personalization

Customizing sauces allows you to tailor flavors to your palate or dietary needs. Whether it's reducing sugar, enhancing spice, or substituting ingredients, the result is uniquely yours.

2. Creativity and Expression

Creating signature sauces is a form of culinary art, blending inspiration with technique to craft memorable dishes.

3. Expanding Your Culinary Repertoire

Exploring new ingredients and techniques keeps your cooking fresh and exciting, whether it's incorporating exotic spices or experimenting with plant-based alternatives.

The Foundations of Sauce Customization

1. Balancing Flavor Profiles

A great sauce balances five key taste elements:

1. Sweet: Honey, sugar, maple syrup, or fruit.
2. Salty: Salt, soy sauce, or fish sauce.
3. Sour: Vinegars, citrus juice, or tamarind.
4. Bitter: Coffee, dark chocolate, or bitter greens.
5. Umami: Parmesan, miso, mushrooms, or anchovies.

Pro Tip: Taste your sauce after each adjustment, layering flavors gradually until the balance feels just right.

2. Adjusting Consistency

The texture of a sauce is as important as its flavor. Adjust consistency to suit its purpose:

- Thickeners: Use cornstarch, flour, or pureed vegetables for a thicker sauce.
- Thin it Out: Add water, broth, or milk for a lighter texture.
- Aeration: Whip or blend for a light, airy sauce.

Pro Tip: Start with small amounts when adding thickeners or liquids to avoid overcorrecting.

3. Enhancing Aromatics

Aromatics like garlic, onions, shallots, and herbs elevate sauces by adding depth and complexity.

- Raw Aromatics: Sharp and pungent, ideal for bold sauces.
- Cooked Aromatics: Mellow and sweet, perfect for creamy or rich sauces.

Pro Tip: Toast or sauté spices and aromatics before incorporating them into the sauce for enhanced flavor.

Creating Your Own Signature Sauces

1. Start with a Base

Every great sauce begins with a solid base:

- Creamy Bases: Mayonnaise, yogurt, or coconut milk for rich dressings.
- Oil-Based: Olive oil or sesame oil for vinaigrettes.

- Broth-Based: Chicken, beef, or vegetable stock for savory sauces.

Pro Tip: Use neutral bases, like cream or plain yogurt, to let your added flavors shine.

2. Experiment with Flavors

- Sweeteners: Try unconventional options like date syrup, agave, or molasses.
- Acids: Explore rice vinegar, balsamic, or citrus zest.
- Spices: Mix familiar spices with bold newcomers like za'atar, sumac, or harissa.

3. Add a Personal Touch

Signature sauces often have a unique ingredient or technique:
- Infused Oils: Use garlic- or herb-infused oils for extra flavor.
- Fermented Additions: Add kimchi juice, miso, or fermented chili paste for umami depth.
- Unexpected Twists: Incorporate peanut butter, tahini, or roasted fruits for a surprising flavor profile.

Pro Tip: Keep notes on your experiments to refine your recipes over time.

Global Influences in Sauce Innovation

1. Asian Inspiration

- Soy Sauce Variations: Combine with ginger, sesame oil, and honey for a simple glaze.
- Miso: Adds richness to creamy sauces and dressings.
- Sambal Oelek: Incorporate this Indonesian chili paste for heat and depth.
Example Sauce: Japanese Ponzu
- Ingredients: Soy sauce, citrus juice, mirin, and dashi.
- Use: Drizzle over grilled fish or vegetables.

2. Mediterranean and Middle Eastern Flavors

- Herbs: Incorporate fresh parsley, cilantro, and dill.
- Tahini: A sesame seed paste perfect for creamy, nutty dressings.

- Pomegranate Molasses: Adds a sweet-tart flavor to vinaigrettes and glazes.
Example Sauce: Harissa Yogurt Sauce
- Ingredients: Greek yogurt, harissa, lemon juice, and olive oil.
- Use: Serve with roasted vegetables or grilled meats.

3. Latin American Flair

- Citrus: Lime and orange add brightness to marinades and dressings.
- Chilies: Experiment with chipotle, guajillo, or ancho chilies for smoky heat.
- Achiote: Adds earthy flavor and vibrant color to sauces.
Example Sauce: Chimichurri
- Ingredients: Parsley, garlic, red wine vinegar, and olive oil.
- Use: Pair with grilled steak or roasted potatoes.

4. African and Caribbean Boldness

- Spices: Use berbere, allspice, or curry powders for warmth and complexity.
- Fruits: Mango, papaya, or pineapple for tropical sweetness.
- Heat: Scotch bonnet peppers for fiery sauces.
Example Sauce: Mango Habanero Glaze
- Ingredients: Pureed mango, habanero peppers, lime juice, and honey.
- Use: Glaze chicken wings or pork chops.

Advanced Techniques for Sauce Crafting

1. Reductions and Concentrations

Simmer sauces to reduce liquid and intensify flavors:
- Wine Reductions: Use red or white wine with aromatics for a glossy finish.
- Balsamic Reduction: Cook balsamic vinegar with sugar until syrupy.
Pro Tip: Use low heat and stir frequently to prevent scorching.

2. Infusions

Infusing oils, vinegars, or cream adds subtle, layered flavors:
- Herbs: Basil or thyme in olive oil.
- Spices: Star anise or cinnamon in cream.
- Citrus: Lemon peel in vinegar.

3. Layering Flavors

Build depth by cooking in stages:
- Sauté aromatics first.
- Add liquids and simmer.
- Finish with fresh herbs or butter for a glossy texture.

Tips for Perfecting Your Sauces

1. Taste Constantly
Taste at every stage to adjust flavors as needed.
2. Keep It Fresh
Add fresh herbs, citrus juice, or zest just before serving for brightness.
3. Avoid Overcomplicating
Too many ingredients can muddle flavors. Aim for balance and simplicity.

Storing and Repurposing Sauces

- Refrigeration: Store in airtight containers for up to one week.
- Freezing: Freeze sauces like pesto or curry paste in ice cube trays for convenience.
- Repurposing: Use leftover sauces as marinades, dips, or soup bases.

Closing Thoughts

Creating your own signature sauces is an exciting journey that blends technique with creativity. By mastering the art of balancing flavors, adjusting textures, and drawing inspiration from global cuisines, you can craft sauces that elevate your cooking to new heights. Experiment boldly, refine your recipes, and let your sauces become a true reflection of your culinary style. Let's continue exploring the endless possibilities of sauce-making and discover what unique flavors you can bring to the table!

Conclusion: Mastering the Art of Sauces and Dressings

Sauces and dressings are the heart of culinary creativity, capable of turning the simplest ingredients into extraordinary meals. They are more than just accompaniments; they are the flavor foundation, the visual appeal, and often the reason we savor every bite. Mastering the art of sauces and dressings is not just about following recipes but about embracing experimentation, discovering your preferences, and developing your unique culinary voice.

In this concluding chapter, we celebrate the transformative power of sauces, encourage you to take risks in the kitchen, and inspire you to continue creating flavors that elevate every dish.

The Power of Sauces and Dressings

1. Transforming the Ordinary into the Extraordinary

Sauces and dressings have the unique ability to breathe new life into everyday ingredients.

- Simple Salads: A well-crafted vinaigrette can turn a basic bowl of greens into a gourmet experience.

- Plain Proteins: Grilled chicken or fish becomes a masterpiece with the addition of a flavorful marinade or creamy sauce.

- Vegetables: Roasted or steamed vegetables shine with a drizzle of herbaceous dressing or nutty glaze.

Example: Imagine a plain roasted potato. Now top it with a garlic aioli or a dollop of chimichurri, and you've created something memorable.

Pro Tip: Think of sauces and dressings as the final seasoning for your dish, tying all elements together.

2. A Gateway to Global Cuisines

Sauces are often the defining feature of a cuisine, capturing the essence of a region's flavors and traditions. By mastering a variety of sauces, you gain access to a world of culinary possibilities:

- French: Hollandaise, béchamel, and velouté.
- Italian: Pesto, marinara, and carbonara.
- Asian: Soy-based sauces, peanut dressings, and curry pastes.
- Latin American: Mole, chimichurri, and salsa verde.

Pro Tip: Use sauces as a way to explore unfamiliar cuisines and ingredients. A single sauce can inspire an entire meal.

3. Elevating Your Cooking Confidence

When you master sauces and dressings, you gain confidence in your cooking. The ability to create flavors, adjust textures, and balance ingredients empowers you to approach any dish with creativity and skill.

Benefits:

- Adaptability: You can tailor sauces to complement any dish or occasion.
- Versatility: Many sauces double as marinades, dips, or finishing drizzles.
- Expression: Crafting your signature sauce becomes an extension of your personality.

Encouragement to Experiment and Innovate

1. Start with the Basics

Every great chef begins with the fundamentals. Practice classic sauces like béchamel, vinaigrette, and hollandaise to understand their structure and components. Once you're comfortable, use them as a springboard for innovation.

Pro Tip: Experiment with adding herbs, spices, or citrus to classic recipes for a personal twist.

2. Embrace Mistakes

Not every sauce will be perfect on the first try, and that's okay. Some of the best discoveries come from happy accidents.

- Lumpy Gravy? Strain it and move on.
- Too Thin? Reduce it or add a thickener.
- Too Bland? Adjust the seasoning with acid, salt, or sweetness.

Pro Tip: Keep tasting as you cook, and don't be afraid to pivot.

3. Customize for Your Taste

Sauces are inherently flexible. Adjust flavors to suit your preferences or dietary needs:

- Substitute Greek yogurt for mayonnaise in creamy dressings for a lighter option.
- Use maple syrup instead of honey for a vegan-friendly sweetener.
- Add fresh chilies or hot sauce to give mild sauces a spicy kick.

4. Experiment with New Ingredients

- Spices: Introduce exotic flavors like za'atar, garam masala, or sumac.
- Herbs: Combine unconventional herbs like tarragon, Thai basil, or shiso.
- Sweeteners: Use agave, molasses, or coconut sugar for unique notes.

Pro Tip: Keep a journal of your experiments to track what works and what doesn't.

The Importance of Sauces in Memorable Meals

1. Creating Harmony

A well-made sauce brings harmony to a dish, tying together diverse flavors and textures. Whether it's the umami of a miso glaze or the tang of a lemon vinaigrette, sauces act as the glue that holds a meal together.

Example: Think of a Thanksgiving dinner without gravy. It wouldn't be the same, as the gravy binds the turkey, stuffing, and potatoes into a cohesive experience.

2. Enhancing Presentation

Sauces are also a visual element, adding color, shine, and elegance to a dish. A simple drizzle, dollop, or smear can make your meal look restaurant-worthy.

Pro Tip: Use a squeeze bottle or a spoon to artfully plate sauces.

3. Unlocking Nostalgia and Emotion

Certain sauces evoke powerful memories and emotions. A bowl of spaghetti with marinara might remind you of childhood dinners, while a tangy barbecue sauce might transport you to summer cookouts. By mastering these sauces, you create the opportunity to craft meaningful experiences for yourself and others.

Practical Tips for Continued Exploration

1. Build a Pantry for Sauces

Keep a well-stocked pantry with essential ingredients like oils, vinegars, mustard, soy sauce, and spices. A prepared pantry ensures you're always ready to whip up a sauce on the fly.

2. Learn from Global Cuisines

Study the techniques and flavors of different regions to broaden your sauce repertoire.

- Italian: Experiment with tomato-based sauces and pestos.

- Asian: Try soy-ginger glazes, hoisin-based sauces, and Thai peanut dressings.

- Middle Eastern: Explore tahini-based dressings or yogurt sauces with za'atar.

3. Pair Sauces with Dishes Thoughtfully

Consider the dish's main ingredients and preparation method when choosing a sauce.

- Rich Proteins: Balance with acidic or tangy sauces (e.g., chimichurri for steak).

- Delicate Fish: Pair with light, citrus-based sauces.

- Hearty Vegetables: Add depth with creamy or spiced sauces.

Final Thoughts and Inspiration

Mastering the art of sauces and dressings is a lifelong journey filled with endless possibilities. The beauty of sauce-making lies in its blend of precision and creativity—measured techniques paired with imaginative flair. By understanding the fundamentals and embracing experimentation, you can transform your meals into unforgettable culinary experiences.

Remember:

- Start with the basics, but don't be afraid to innovate.

- Taste and adjust as you go, trusting your instincts.

- Draw inspiration from global cuisines to keep your cooking fresh and exciting.

Sauces and dressings are the ultimate tool for expression in the kitchen. They are your signature, your secret ingredient, and your way of turning the everyday into the extraordinary. So, pick up your whisk, grab a handful of fresh herbs, and dive into the endless world of sauce-making. Your culinary adventure awaits!

Don't miss out!

Visit the website below and you can sign up to receive emails whenever Olivia Bennett publishes a new book. There's no charge and no obligation.

https://books2read.com/r/B-A-QLEKD-NEEAG

BOOKS 2 READ

Connecting independent readers to independent writers.

About the Author

Olivia Bennett is a celebrated food writer and chef with expertise spanning multiple culinary disciplines. With a passion for making home cooking accessible, she specializes in guiding readers through everything from hearty casseroles to delicate pastries. Her work is known for its clear instructions, practical tips, and deep understanding of both traditional and modern cooking techniques.